DATE DUE

Jackie Robinson
and the Integration
of Baseball

TURNING POINTS

Preeminent writers offering fresh, personal
perspectives on the defining events of our time

Published Titles

William Least Heat-Moon, *Columbus in the Americas*
Scott Simon, *Jackie Robinson and the
Integration of Baseball*

Forthcoming Titles

Douglas Brinkley on the March on Washington
William F. Buckley Jr. on the Fall of the Berlin Wall
Eleanor Clift on Passing the 19th Amendment
Alan Dershowitz on the Declaration of Independence
Thomas Fleming on the Louisiana Purchase
Sir Martin Gilbert on D-Day

TURNING POINTS

Jackie Robinson
and the Integration of Baseball

SCOTT SIMON

John Wiley & Sons, Inc.

Published by John Wiley & Sons, Inc., Hoboken, New Jersey
Published simultaneously in Canada

Design and production by Navta Associates, Inc.

For general information about our other products and services, please contact our Customer Care Department within the United States at (800) 762-2974, outside the United States at (317) 572-3993 or fax (317) 572-4002.

Wiley also publishes its books in a variety of electronic formats. Some content that appears in print may not be available in electronic books.

ISBN 0-471-26153-X

Printed in the United States of America

10 9 8 7 6 5 4 3 2 1

For New York

Contents

1

Hero

As I began this book, many Americans were beginning to be cautious about whom they called a hero. Athletes, actors, entrepreneurs, and celebrities had casually and carelessly been described as such. To do so after September 11, 2001, seemed preposterous. In the weeks following the attacks on New York and Washington, D.C., and the foiled attack that sent a plane crashing into western Pennsylvania, Americans saw the grim and affecting faces of genuine heroes— and they were caked in ash, blood, tears, toil, and sweat.

A man or woman might sink a basketball, strike a baseball, or scintillate before a camera lens. Those talents can be worthy. But real heroes risk their lives for others.

My wife and I were crossing midtown Manhattan about three weeks after the attacks and saw an assemblage of broad shoulders in blue uniforms with red patches standing outside the entrance to a church. The men and women talked softly; anonymous black cars thrummed their motors softly; pink and white flowers were piled softly into the crooks of the concrete stairs. It was the funeral for a New York firefighter. We went inside, impulsively, and then stayed, decisively. Gerard Barbara, who was a fifty-three-year-old assistant chief of the Fire Department of New York, had died risking his life for strangers. It did not seem strange—in fact, it seemed important—to take a seat amid some of the men and women who had loved him. They wore blue uniforms, thick-soled black shoes, and red eyes. Mayor Giuliani got up to speak, a gravelly voiced man in a gray suit, who also had red eyes. It was Mayor Giuliani's fourth funeral service of the day.

"Your father," he said to Gerard Barbara's son and daughter, "used his great gift of courage to serve others. The name he gave you," he continued in the blunt tone of a commandment, "is now a permanent part of the history of this city. And now, I would like everyone here to stand and express their appreciation for your father." We stood, cried, and clapped our hands until our palms burned like our eyes, then we applauded some more. A line of blue shoulders with red patches filed softly out of the church and back onto Fifth Avenue, where, for at least a time, FDNY had replaced DKNY as a signature of distinction.

The following weekend, we watched Cal Ripken Jr. play his last game of major league baseball—his 3,001st.

Over a quarter of a century as a professional athlete, Cal Ripken had become such an insignia of sturdiness and class that the umpires stood in a line to shake his hand. His opponents removed their fielding gloves to applaud him. The signs blooming amid the green seats of Baltimore's Oriole Park at Camden Yards said WE LOVE YOU CAL; THANKS, CAL; and CAL: WE'LL NEVER FORGET YOU. But the word *hero* seemed conspicuously, deliberately absent. Events had revised our national vocabulary. At least for the moment—it would be nice to think even for longer—it would be hard for Americans to look out at a mere playing field and see the kind of heroism we had been reminded to revere in men and women in blue uniforms with red patches.

But even by this wiser standard, Jackie Robinson was a hero. The baseball diamond is not simply a playing field in his story. It was the ground on which he was most open and vulnerable to taunts, threats, and sharpened spikes.

The first African American major league ballplayer of the twentieth century routinely took his rolling, pigeon-toed stride out into the infield or batter's box on days and nights when local police had culled the stadium's mail to show him an assortment of explicit and persuasive death threats. It is tempting today, when Jackie Robinson is enshrined in halls of fame, social studies curricula,

3

classroom calendars, songs, and statues, to suppose those threats were empty. But in the late 1940s, beatings, bombings, lynchings, and shootings scarred the landscape of the United States. They could be just as public as— well, as baseball games.

Jackie Robinson gave his life for something great; heroes do. He chose to bear the daily, bloody trial of standing up to beanballs and cleats launched into his shins, chest, and chin, and the race-baiting taunts raining down from the stands, along with trash, tomatoes, rocks, watermelon slices, and Sambo dolls. And then he performed with eloquent achievement and superlative poise. Robinson allowed that hatred to strike him as it would a lightning rod, chanelling it down into the rugged earth of himself. All that America saw for many years on the baseball field was that iron as upright as a steeple, never bending. But inside, the strain slowed his body, whitened his hair, thickened his circulation, aggravated his diabetes, and rendered him slow and blind. He was dead by the age of fifty-three—a martyr (a word as deliberately applied as *hero*) to trying to make America live up to its creed.

If Jackie Robinson had not been selected to play the role he performed so well, no doubt other superb African American athletes would have soon stepped onto the stage. The skills of Larry Doby, Roy Campanella, Sam Jethroe, Ray Dandridge, Willie Mays, Monte Irvin, Ernie Banks, and an aging Satchel Paige were too great not to tempt major league clubs who were searching for new sources of talent. World War II had moved many Americans to examine their nation's own self-image as a bulwark of freedom. Editorial writers and civic leaders were already clamoring for America to integrate the armed forces, which had just won the world's liberty, the schools, in which children learned about justice, and sports, which purported to epitomize American values. How could a young black man who might be called up to risk his life backing up Pee Wee Reese in Guam, or Yogi Berra in Normandy, not be allowed to earn a living alongside them on the same playing field?

America's modern civil rights revolution was already stirring by the time Jackie Robinson arrived in major league baseball. With Vernon Johns, Thurgood Marshall, A. Philip Randolph, and many more, it had already produced heroes. But Robinson's courage and accomplishment put a familiar face on the kind of bravery that it took for blacks to stand up for their rights. His heroism was no greater than that of millions of others—some achievements simply cannot fit into box scores. But Robinson's renown gave his heroism reach. It is possible to see, in Robinson's slow, purposeful walk into the face of taunts and threats, some of the same unbowed courage that Americans would later admire in the civil rights marchers who faced down stinging water sprays, sharp rocks, and snapping police dogs. When Robinson joined Dr. Martin Luther King's nonviolent campaign in

Birmingham in 1963, marchers called out, "Show us, Jackie!"

Jackie Robinson is so highly esteemed for his Gandhian restraint against the onslaughts of bigotry that it is easy to mistake him for a social activist. He certainly became a militant campaigner for civil rights, an outspoken newspaper columnist, and a combative Republican when that party was more identified among blacks with Lincoln, La Guardia, Rockefeller, and Lindsay, while the Democrats were dishonored by Strom Thurmond, Orville Faubus, and George Wallace.

But first and last, Jackie Robinson was a hard-nosed, hard-assed, brass-balled, fire-breathing athlete. The Jackie Robinson that his old Pasadena and UCLA teammates remembered could be a petulant star. He mocked lesser competitors and came to expect that his regal status on fields of play would excuse him from the need to attend class or complete assignments; and so it did. When, on a couple of occasions, Robinson's high spirits and dark skin brought him into the grasp of the Pasadena police, his case was considered with compassion by a local judge, who was loath to deliver a penalty that would cause the accused to miss next Saturday's game. Few other young black men in Southern California could rally so effective a defense as Robinson's in rushing yards, passes caught, and punts returned.

Jackie Robinson played less than a single season in the Negro Leagues, for the fabled Kansas City Monarchs.

Among a group of gifted professionals who had to endure all-night rides on bone-clattering buses and blocked doors at whites-only diners and motels, Jackie Robinson was remembered more for griping about the league's showboating and lack of training and discipline. He let his teammates know that he considered the league beneath his talents (and maybe it was—for all of them).

The Jackie Robinson who stayed on to become a perennial major league star after he became a hero could be prickly. Another way to say it is: Jackie Robinson could be a prick. Even after he had become one of the most admired personalities in America, Robinson could spring up and cry racism at umpires with the impudence to call him out on a close slide or a strike. He could crash into an opponent's knees on inconsequential plays, just to let them know he could hurt them. He harangued opposing players, and sometimes his own teammates, with graphic epithets of the kind that would have once been considered legal provocation for a duel (although the epithets were never racial and rarely sexual—Jackie Robinson was no racist, and he was even a bit of a prude).

But Jackie Robinson was no less a hero for being a full-blooded human being. When he was summoned by history, he risked his safety and sanity to give history the last full measure of his strength, nerve, and perseverance. In the end, real heroes give us stories we use to reinforce our own lives.

• • •

Shortly before nine o'clock on the morning of September 11, 2001, Jackie Robinson's widow, Rachel Robinson, and Dorothy and Mark Reese, Pee Wee Reese's widow and son, were in New York's City Hall, along with old Dodgers Ralph Branca and Joe Black. They were there to choose among five sculptor's models arrayed on a conference table, each depicting that fabled moment from the 1947 season in which Pee Wee Reese had crossed the field from his post at shortstop during a downpour of racial taunts to slip his arm encouragingly around Jackie Robinson's shoulders.

Before the group could choose a model to be cast in bronze and put up in Brooklyn, they heard a boom, then a commotion. New York police officers rushed them onto a bus. The bus got blocked and could not move through the tangle in the streets. New police officers sprinted aboard and took the Dodger family members into the bomb shelter of a nearby bank building, which is where they were, huddled and held rapt before a television set, when the first World Trade tower fell from the skyline. Dorothy Reese turned to her son, who is a California filmmaker. "I'm just glad," she said in the first gloom of the attack, "that Jackie and your father aren't here to see this." Mark Reese gently, consolingly, disagreed. "I think Pee Wee and Jackie are here," he told his mother. "And we need their courage now." I can't think of a time when we don't.

The story of Jackie Robinson's arrival in the major leagues is a heroic American legend. It is not in the same rank as Valley Forge, Gettysburg, Lincoln's trials, Harriet Tubman's bravery, Chief Joseph's valor, or the gallantry of the police and firefighters who ran willingly into the firestorm of the World Trade Center. But Jackie Robinson's story still testifies to the power of pure personal courage to turn history and transform adversaries into admirers. It is a story that endures all the nicks and nits of revisionism because, when the last page is turned, it plays on in our minds and lives: a bold man, dark-skinned and adorned in Dodger blue, who displays the daring and audacity to stand unflinchingly against taunts, strike back at beanballs, and steal home with fifty thousand people watching and waiting for *Jackie Robinson* to spring willingly into the path of a pitched ball and slide into the ironbound clench of a catcher protecting home plate. It is a story that still rouses us to shake off dust, blood, and bruises and *keep going*.

2

Steaming Home

At the close of World War II, the United States was both a citadel of freedom and a bastion of segregation.

Americans had been slow to see any threat to their own freedom in the rising menaces of Nazism and Japanese imperialism. Many Americans had been more or less willing to see the old monarchies of Europe squeezed between two tyrants, and Asia overrun by strutting militarists. But the attack on Pearl Harbor shook Americans out of their sleepy self-absorption. They then gave their muscle and treasure to throwing back oppression across the world. They sent their own sons (and more than a few daughters) from Nebraska and Oregon to Normandy and Iwo Jima. They shed their own blood on forlorn European bluffs and a score of Pacific islands and atolls.

But the forces of soldiers and sailors that represented America were profoundly segregated. Whites, blacks, and Japanese Americans (who were recruited into their separate brigades) wore the same uniform, and fought for the same flag. But they served, slept, ate, and even waged war in separate units. The black seamen who loaded the bombs onto the boats that steamed into battle often welcomed assignment away from home, to England and Australia. At least there they could buy a beer in a pub without signs that said "No Colored Allowed."

During the years in which America prevented racist tyrannies from engulfing Europe and Asia, twenty-one black citizens were strung up from trees in Alabama, Mississippi, Georgia, and Louisiana. Those were just the lynchings that were reported: public events, with crowds, cameras, and even picnics. Clergymen often attended, to sanctify the proceedings. There were also scores of racial murders that local police declined to consider crimes: beatings, shootings, and firebombs tossed into bedroom windows of black families in the middle of the night.

At the close of World War II, no major nation in the world was freer or stronger than the United States. But few major nations so openly and legally subjugated so many of its own citizens. When the National Party came to power in South Africa in 1948, it had a model for designing the particulars of the racial division it called *apartheid:* the American South, and the comprehensive array of signs that hung over schools, rest rooms, restaurants, water fountains, soda fountain counters, movie theaters, and even churches:

WHITES ONLY

NO COLORED

Such signs are almost impossible to imagine today. Museums have been opened so that we don't forget their ugliness and cruelty, the way those signs disfigured a free society. But a half-century ago, many Americans found it impossible to imagine living in a place that wasn't so marked.

In July 1944, Army lieutenant Jack Robinson defied those lines when he got aboard a bus on the Fort Hood army base in Texas and took a seat in a middle row. The unwritten rule of Texas transit then was that whites could fill the rows in the front of the bus until they were all seated. Blacks could only take seats beginning from the back. But the unmarked line between front and back moved back and forth like the first-down chain on a football field, as white riders came on and got off. The lunatic fine points of official segregation were clear to bigots: no black man or woman could take a seat in front of a white, or in the same row; on no account could blacks and whites ever sit next to one another.

The U.S. Army had banned segregation on buses that operated on army bases in 1944, after uniformed soldiers Joe Louis and Sugar Ray Robinson had famously refused to be relegated to a segregated area of an Alabama bus depot. The army was mortified. Louis and Robinson were on morale-building tours of army bases. Their mission was to shake hands in hospitals, barracks, and dining halls, and box a few desultory exhibition rounds with local palookas who would wear a small plum of a bruise as a medal from the great Louis or Robinson. The champions' visits were supposed to remind the soldiers of Jesse Owens outrunning Hitler's brownshirts at the Munich Olympics* and Joe Louis conquering Max Schmeling—of America's bashing equality, not its appalling racism.

Jackie Robinson had confronted little in the U.S. Army that would convince an intelligent man that the uniform he wore signified that his side was battling for liberty. After filling the Rose Bowl on Sunday afternoons playing football for UCLA, the U.S. Army put Jackie Robinson in segregated barracks. At Fort Riley, Kansas, he was denied the chance to qualify for officer training that his academic and athletic background should have conferred—and did, on white men. Robinson complained to Joe Louis, who also happened to be stationed there; he mentioned the affront to an adviser in the White House, who contacted the Pentagon. Public affairs officers interceded with Fort Riley's commanders to explain that keeping the most renowned college athlete in the country out of the officer corps would bestow no

---

* Mack Robinson, Jackie's older brother, finished second behind Jessie Owens and won a silver medal for the United States.

acclaim on either the army or themselves. So Robinson was commissioned a lieutenant. Grudgingly.

Lieutenant Robinson was then appointed a morale officer for black soldiers at Fort Hood. The morale officer was traditionally in charge of keeping his unit stocked with ample amenities and diversions, from chewing gum to condoms to Friday night movies. The army suggested that the morale of Robinson's unit would be enriched if Lieutenant Robinson became a running back for Fort Hood's football team, which played local colleges as well as other army bases. But Robinson did not want to spend sweltering Texas afternoons bouncing lesser athletes off his All-American knees. He refused.

His rebuff grew more resolute when Robinson presented himself at Fort Hood's dusty baseball diamond and asked to try out for the baseball team. He was turned away—told to his face by a fellow officer, a white man, that "you have to play for the colored team." It was an unfunny joke: there was no colored team. After a fabled college career during which he was laden with honors, cheers, entreaties from coeds of all colors, and emoluments from alumni, this moment might have been the first time that Jackie Robinson ran across organized segregation on a sports field. The notion that some people might care more about ethnicity than victory was outlandish to Robinson. Pete Reiser, who would later be Robinson's teammate on the Brooklyn Dodgers, was also stationed at Fort Hood and was present that day on the diamond. He remembered Robinson stalking off with his glove on his hip, his face flushed and furious. Five years later that face would become a famous American image: a brave man walking nobly away from bigotry. But at the time, Reiser thought that Robinson looked like a man swallowing a scream.

No black man in the United States of 1942 needed army service to make him conscious of America's racial shortcomings and crimes. But few men of his age could have had the breadth of Robinson's experience of being at once sought after and acclaimed for his athletic skill and rejected for his color.* Confronting racism in the army sharpened the social consciousness of a college athlete who may have grown to believe that his playing talents had enabled him to outrun racial hate. And it *sharpened* him.

As a morale officer at Fort Hood, Robinson fielded complaints about the limited number of stools on which black soldiers and their families were permitted to sit at the base's segregated soda fountain: four, and on the side of the fountain adjoining a grill. The dozen seats spanning the front of the fountain were reserved for whites. A black soldier, bone-weary from maneuvers, would have to

---

* Except for Mack Robinson, who returned with his silver medal from the Olympic Games to a parade in Pasadena, and then was enjoined from any city job except garbage collector. And when black sanitation workers won a court judgment for equal pay, they were fired.

stand and wait for one of the four to become open. His pregnant wife or rambunctious son would have to wait while whites sprang up and departed, leaving open seats.

Jackie Robinson called a base officer to propose that the allotment for blacks be increased to at least six. But this would entail lengthening the black section so that it curved around to the front of the soda fountain. It opened the possibility that a white might take that last seat before the black section began, order a milk shake, and find a black man or woman sitting next to him.

Robinson's first call was to a Major Hafner, who apparently did not recognize his name from sports and had not seen him in person. He must have known that the 761st Tank Battalion was a black unit, but assumed that Lt. Jack R. Robinson was a white officer assigned to oversee their morale. The officer bridled at the proposal to increase the number of seats for blacks; he seemed to grasp at once that it would open the possibility of blacks taking seats next to whites.

"Lieutenant Robinson," the major exclaimed over the base telephone, "let me put it this way. Would you like it if your wife had to sit next to a nigger?"

Robinson had been a storied broken-field runner at UCLA. But on hearing this question, he chose a direct attack across the line. "Godammit," said Jackie Robinson, "I *am* a Negro officer, and how in the hell do you know that your wife hasn't already been with a Negro?"

The number of seats for blacks was increased to six.

• • •

Jackie Robinson did not board that bus late on a summer's night determined to disobey official segregation. He had been undergoing examination at a hospital thirty miles off the base, so that doctors could inspect the ankle he had turned while playing intercollegiate football. Robinson needed the doctors to certify that he could be deployed overseas with his 761st Tank Battalion as the Allied troops drove toward Berlin. Robinson had left the hospital on the evening of July 6, 1944, to while away about three hours at the Negro officers club. Close to midnight, he boarded a Fort Hood bus that would take him back to his hospital quarters.

Robinson had actually started to move unquestioningly to the rear of the bus when he saw a friend sitting four rows from the back of the bus. She was Virginia Jones, the wife of a fellow officer, Gordon Jones. There were no other blacks aboard the bus, nor, so far as has ever been reported, were there any Mexicans, who were then subject to the same casual maliciousness of race laws.

The bus had traveled about half a dozen blocks before the driver, a local civilian named Milton Renegar, noticed Robinson sitting next to Mrs. Jones and called back to him, "You got to move back, boy." Mrs. Jones, it becomes essential to report, was a light-skinned woman. The driver seems to have assumed that she was white. In the statement that she later offered officials, Virginia

Jones made a point of saying that she had taken a seat four rows from the back of the bus, "which I always thought was the back of the bus." And so it was—unless the bus was so crowded that a white person wanted to sit there. Then the back of the bus would not begin until three rows from the back. What Milton Renegar thought he had seen in his overhead mirror was a broad-shouldered black army lieutenant brazenly take a seat next to a white woman. He told an inquiry that he said, "You, next to that woman. You got to move back, boy."

Robinson did not move. He did not incline his head to hear the driver; he did not scowl or stare down at the floor, like an upbraided child. Instead, he stared out of the bus window with sharp and almost theatrical carelessness. A four-letter college athlete from the golden suburbs of Southern California and an officer in the U.S. Army, he was not about to be ordered around by a small-town Texas bus driver.

The driver stopped the bus. He couldn't drive on, he said—it was a violation of the law to have a black man sitting so close to the front of his bus. Robinson replied, evenly, that military regulations were clear: he was free to sit wherever a seat was open. White voices began to clamor, some telling Robinson to move, others calling for the driver to move on, let the boy be, they had places to go, just drive on and call the police when they stopped at the bus depot. After half an hour, they reached the terminal. The driver ran off to report that a colored man had refused to move to the back of the bus. Robinson and Mrs. Jones began to wait for a second bus to complete their rides home. White men from the first bus gathered around them, muttering and flexing their arms. The bus driver returned with his supervisor; Lieutenant Robinson shook a finger in his face, struggling to keep his sentence short and pointed: "Quit fucking with me," he said. A woman who had been aboard the bus, perhaps emboldened by the growing crowd of white men, then shook her finger in Robinson's face and fairly spat out the word: *"Nigger."*

Military police arrived. They suggested that Robinson go with them to the provost marshal's office, perhaps as much to avoid gathering a crowd on a small-town Texas street as to bring Robinson in to account for the incident. Pointedly, perhaps, the MPs did not arrest a U.S. Army officer whose unit was training for deployment overseas. And they waited for Mrs. Jones to safely board her next bus.

By the time Robinson was delivered to military police headquarters, he was righteously angry. He felt that he had conducted himself as an officer and a man. He had upheld military regulations aboard the bus, and was now being asked to answer for it. A private at MP headquarters asked if Robinson was "the nigger lieutenant" that they had brought in. Robinson told Pvt. Ben Mucklerath, "If you ever call me a nigger again, I'll break you

in two." The private looked at the strapping and angry
lieutenant and seemed to remember he was armed with
only a baton and a revolver. He ran off to report the
affront to Capt. Gerald Bear, the assistant provost marshal who would question Robinson. When Robinson
overheard the private dramatizing their encounter
(Robinson thought he had issued a guarantee, not a
threat; it needed no elaboration), the captain told the
lieutenant to be quiet—and not to be "so uppity." A
white stenographer, a local woman named Mrs. Wilson,
arrived. She took it upon herself to interrupt Captain
Bear's interrogation to tell Robinson, "Don't you know
you have no right to sit up there in the white part of that
bus?" The statement she transcribed still bristles with
Robinson's explicit and unapologetic contempt for the
driver, the passengers, the army, the lady who called him
a nigger, the private who called him a nigger, the captain
who called him uppity, the stenographer who chastened
him as if he were a misguided child, the entire hot and
humiliating small-town Southern experience.

"He [the driver] told the people, 'This nigger is making trouble,'" Robinson remembered. "I told the bus
driver to stop fucking with me. So he gets the rest of the
men around there and starts blowing his top and someone calls the MPs. Outside of telling this lady [the white
woman at the bus station] that I didn't care if she
preferred charges against me or not, I was speaking

direct to that bus driver. And just as I told the captain here [Bear], if any one of you called me a nigger, I would do the same."

Robinson was court-martialed—not for refusing to move to the back of a bus (army regulations rather clearly supported him there), but for being truculent to the officer who questioned him, and for swearing ("insubordinate, disrespectful, and discourteous").

During the month in which he awaited his court appearance, Robinson made certain that his case was reported to the NAACP, both of California's senators, sports reporters at black newspapers who had covered his college career, and the Secretary of War. By the time the court-martial was convened, stories in the black press of New York, Chicago, Pittsburgh, and Los Angeles had upbraided the army for prosecuting a former four-letter athlete for UCLA, the brother of an Olympic medal winner, for asserting his rights under the army's own regulations.

Within four hours, Jackie Robinson was acquitted. His unit was soon thereafter sent overseas. But Robinson did not join them. His injured ankle got him assigned to "permanent limited duty," and Robinson invoked the lingering celebrity of his undergraduate athletic career to lobby with Pentagon officers to get discharged outright. Jackie Robinson was a star, not the sort of man you assigned to "permanent limited duty."

The army was agreeable. In fact, it seemed relieved.

They cut an order saying Lt. Jack Roosevelt Robinson was "honorably relieved from active duty." It was an honorable discharge, but barely; it did not include veterans' benefits, even as it recognized that Robinson's ankle was unfit for full deployment.*

The discharge amounted to a no-fault divorce. Robinson had become classified as an official aggravation, an agitator who would run to heavyweights—of the ring, of the press, in the White House—with his grievances. Robinson, for his part, had experienced only that part of the American military that defended segregation, not the part that battled for freedom. The war in Europe was grinding up lives and shedding blood. Jackie Robinson was not, like Muhammad Ali a generation later, resisting a war he thought was immoral. But he did not resist being relieved from fighting a war overseas when he had already fought his battles at home. The U.S. Army was not inclined to pick any more fights with Jackie Robinson. And Jackie Robinson was not inclined to fight for the United States.

---

* The exclusion of benefits had little effect on Jackie Robinson's life. Robinson did not need veterans' benefits to finance a college education or medical care. But it may be instructive to contemplate what would have become of any other black veteran who developed severe diabetes twenty-five years after his service—and was not eligible for medical care because he had defied segregation laws that were later condemned.

• • •

Military service was a nasty time for Jackie Robinson—segregation, rejection, taunts, and, finally, a court-martial. Robinson's courage was pronounced. He might have talked his way around the confrontation by pointing out to the bus driver that Virginia Jones was black, or telling Captain Bear that he regretted causing any offense to Private Mucklerath or Mrs. Wilson if he had, in the heat of disagreement, objected to being called a nigger. But that would have been a minstrel act. Instead, he chose to keep his seat, stand up against segregation, and invite a court-martial that risked soiling his reputation as a celebrity athlete with the stain of a dishonorable discharge.

If Jackie Robinson had been convicted—even of charges so slight and borderline hysterical as being "insubordinate, disrespectful, and discourteous"—it seems reasonable to assume that Brooklyn's upstanding general manager, Branch Rickey, would have ruled him out of consideration for the role he wanted to cast for a man to break baseball's color barrier. And if Robinson had merely accepted his acquittal, he would have been deployed overseas and risked his life to help win the war in Europe and police the peace.

But being "honorably relieved from active duty" (along with his four-letter college career) put an item in Robinson's career statistics that distinguished him from more experienced Negro League stars who had been too old for military service. The discharge that the army awarded Jackie Robinson to ease his departure also made it possible for Robinson to be wearing the uniform of the Kansas City Monarchs in 1945; other promising black ballplayers were still in army or navy fatigues. They were beyond sight of the scouts Rickey had shipped around the country, charged with finding a black player he could sign to end World War II with an intrepid demonstration that Americans fighting for freedom overseas were now braced to bring liberty and justice home.

In the late autumn of 1945, Pee Wee Reese was steaming home from Guam on a U.S. Navy ship when he heard that a plot of land he regarded as his particular property—the acreage between second and third base in Brooklyn's Ebbets Field—might not be so familiar on his return. A petty officer had heard some news whistling over the shortwave and clanged up a flight of steel stairs to find the ship's best-known sailor.

"Radio says that the Dodgers have hired a colored ballplayer."

The Montreal Royals, Brooklyn's principal farm club, had signed a Negro League player to a major league contract.

· · ·

Pee Wee Reese (a childhood nickname that had stuck; Harold Henry Reese had grown up to 5'10", which was even slightly above the average height for a North American male) was interested, but not astonished. He had played major league baseball for three years before giving three years to the U.S. Navy. He had played in exhibition games against black ballplayers, and the results had been about even. He knew white players who had tried to get a hit off Satchel Paige, and who told Reese that no pitcher on the planet—*none*—was more cunning and accomplished.

The white players who had barnstormed against black clubs accepted the Negro stars as talented performers. But few saw them as potential competitors. The United States was peculiar about race, and while limited integration had penetrated several northern cities, organized baseball was as much its own society as the American military. Many of that society's accents were southern—as was Pee Wee Reese's own rich Kentucky twang.

But Reese was the sort of man and athlete who stayed alert for what was happening in all fields. Even before he left for war, Pee Wee had heard that a few Negro League players had been put through covert tryouts in West Coast minor league ballparks. He knew that a showboat minor league operator named Bill Veeck, the son of the former president of the Chicago Cubs, wanted to buy the Philadelphia Phillies and stock it with aging Negro League stars while younger white major and minor

league players were at war. A team with, say, Satchel
Paige, Josh Gibson, and Ray Dandridge might well have
won a World Series against the elderly 4-Fs who then
stocked major league rosters. But baseball commissioner
Kenesaw Landis disapproved of the idea. He didn't care
for Bill Veeck, he didn't trust his money, and he certainly
didn't endorse his scheme. What if Philadelphia's fans
decided that they liked winning and didn't want to
return to segregated, second-division baseball? The
American way of life could be overturned.

But Pee Wee Reese had played in New York, and he
was not the kind of athlete or celebrity who read the
newspaper just to look for his own name. Even before he
left for the war, several newspapers and civic committees
had called for New York's three major league clubs to
sign black ballplayers. You could not demand that blacks
risk their lives for the United States, they said, without
affording them the same right to earn a living as white
citizens once they returned home. Jesse Owens's gold
medal strides in the 1936 Olympics, and Joe Louis
standing over the felled form of Max Schmeling, had
been sports victories that were taken to signify Germany's
obsession with racial purity.

Reese was a son of the South. His father was a railroad
detective who rode the lines and knew that the Depression, war, lynchings, and race laws had sent trainloads of
blacks north, filling vast blocks of New York, Chicago,
Detroit, and Cleveland. Those cities were the strongholds

27

of major league baseball, and the Dodgers, Giants, White Sox, Cubs, Tigers, and Indians needed black fans to help fill their ballparks.

But Reese was also aware of another calculation: a man could not play baseball for a living without wondering how to beat the New York Yankees. The Yankees were already the preeminent franchise in American sports, a national emblem of New York's imperial status. Every fan outside New York professed to hate them. Every fan in the nation had to be at least a little fascinated by them. There were other teams, and other stars. But the Yankees were the gold standard, the Cadillac, the National Gallery, the Garbo's salary, the cellophane of franchises. Youngsters growing up on the plains of Oklahoma, or the hollers of West Virginia, or a hamlet of New Hampshire who imagined themselves as ballplayers usually envisioned themselves wearing Yankee pinstripes.

The Yankees had won the American League pennant and the World Series for four of the five years immediately preceding America's entry into the war that would put most major league players into service uniforms. The team had spent a few vexing years after the decline of Babe Ruth, and his vintage of Yankees won their last World Series in 1936. But by 1936, the tested and persisting talents of Lou Gehrig and Bill Dickey had been refreshed by the arrival of Joe DiMaggio of Martinez, California. They won the World Series that year, and then again in 1937, 1938, 1939 (Lou Gehrig's last year;

he would die two years later), and 1941.* The Yankees' rich mix of wealth, fame, and the incomparable prominence of playing in New York drew talents like Joe DiMaggio's from clear across the country. DiMaggio would be just thirty years old when he returned from the war in 1945. New York's power to attract excellence seemed destined to proceed undimmed for the rest of the decade. The more championships the Yankees won, the more major league baseball seemed a game divided not so much into leagues as into the Yankees and mere also-rans. *Unless.*

The largest single supply of unsigned baseball talent resided in the Negro Leagues. A major league owner in Brooklyn, St. Louis, or Chicago might not be able to outscout and outspend the Yankees. But he could find and sign gifted ballplayers in places the Yankees ignored. The major league owner with the nerve to try to tap into the vein of talent in the Negro Leagues might strike gold.

Pee Wee Reese was a shortstop. The best shortstops had a sense of anticipation.

"And Pee Wee?"

---

* What happened in 1940? The Detroit Tigers of Hank Greenberg and Charlie Gehringer would beat out the Yankees for the American League pennant, then lose the World Series to a Cincinnati Reds team whose names would ignite few memories today.

Reese waited for the petty officer to add what he had really come to tell him.

"The colored guy is a shortstop."

The news got even better.

"You hear a name?" asked Pee Wee Reese.

"Robinson, I think," said the sailor. "Jack. California."

Pee Wee Reese had even heard—though only heard—about Jack Robinson. He knew that he had been heralded as the most versatile college athlete in the nation (track, baseball, football, and basketball, and all that prevented him from starring on the golf team at UCLA was segregation on golf courses) and was the younger brother of Olympic runner Mack Robinson.

Over the years, as Reese's importance in Jackie Robinson's story and the integration of baseball came to be established and admired, he would feel comfortable enough to tell interviewers about some of the resentments that riled his mind as he tossed about on the troopship steaming home. Major league teams had sent their players off to war with patriotic parades and implied promises that their jobs would be waiting for them on their return. If a sixteen-year-old kid, or a Mennonite pacifist, or someone rejected by the armed forces for having hammertoes, played well in the absence of a major leaguer who had been taken away to defend his country, Reese felt, then a veteran—whether he was a steamfitter, bank clerk, or shortstop—should not have to worry about returning home to find his job filled.

Just below that grudge was another: the shortstop Brooklyn had signed was *a colored guy.*

Reese had played enough exhibition baseball against black teams to have shucked himself of the kind of illusions that comforted racists—that blacks did not know what base to throw to, or were almost comically frightened by beanballs. Reese worried about how three years of naval duty might have battered his baseball skills. He worried that a polished college athlete, a black ballplayer who had spent the war refining his game (for Reese did not know then that Jackie Robinson had refused to play sports for a segregated army), might win the job at shortstop that had belonged to Pee Wee Reese.

In the early 1970s, Reese bluntly re-created his fears for writer Roger Kahn. Actually, a single fear was paramount: "I go back to Louisville. The people say, 'Reese, you weren't man enough to protect your job from a nigger.'"

But Reese also had another trait of a great shortstop: he could project his own fine mind into the skin of an opponent. He imagined how Robinson might feel: "I mean if they said to me, 'Reese, you got to go over and play in the colored guys' league,' how would I feel? Scared. The only white. Lonely. But I'm a good shortstop and that's what I'd want 'em to see. Not my color. Just that I can play the game. And that's how I got to look at Robinson. If he's man enough to take my job, I'm not gonna like it, but dammit, black or white, he deserves it."

Like so many veterans, Pee Wee Reese had already seen a lot of history—lives lost, strewn around, and rearranged utterly. He was not the young man who had gone off to war, and by the time his troopship tied up in San Francisco, he sensed that the game to which he had given his life was about to budge history.

3
Brooklyn, 1947

At the end of World War II, Brooklyn was often regarded as Manhattan's sister among the New York boroughs. Comically plump, a little plain, perhaps—but with an appealing personality. In the way in which siblings find themselves assigned roles in families, Brooklyn was the sidekick to Manhattan's star, a one-word setup to a punch line: "I'm from Brooklyn. And in Brooklyn, we . . ."

Manhattan was the borough of office towers and neon nights, while Brooklyn proclaimed itself the borough of well-attended churches, neatly tended trees, and trolleys. Manhattan was Carnegie Hall, Gershwin, Toscanini, and Duke Ellington's Harlem. Brooklyn was Coney Island, stickball, half-sour dills, and doo-wop.

Manhattan was "the city," where fathers worked, mothers shopped, and children were taken a few times a year to buy a new coat, see a museum or show (although

Brooklyn had outstanding museums, stage shows, and bargain racks), and ride the subway back home. Manhattan was a destination. But Brooklyn was where the city *lived*.

Brooklyn was forlornly incorporated into greater New York in 1898. But it was never quite reconciled to being one of five boroughs of an empire city. In the 1940s, Brooklyn rolled over eighty square miles and was filled with at least thirty distinct neighborhoods and almost three million residents. Had Brooklyn been left contentedly autonomous, it would have rivaled Chicago as America's Second City.

Manhattan, of course, is an island, defined by rugged escarpments and man-made shores, each inch precious for being so scarce. Brooklyn had its own shore along Coney Island and Brighton Beach, but beyond that widened into a vast urban interior that gave much of the borough the feel of an inland city—flat, broad, almost Midwestern. Great ships docked in Manhattan, but they were built in the Brooklyn Navy Yard.

Manhattan had a landscape of towers and skyscrapers that was identifiable in most places around the world. But Brooklyn had its own distinct panorama: church spires and three-story brownstones, small parishes and neighborhood shuls, trolley cables spitting sparks and children leaning out to shout over flower boxes, black-topped school yards and precinct houses, redbrick factories and red-lit corner saloons, bare-chested men in shorts and tall black socks tanning their shoulders while sitting on tar-paper apartment house roofs, and drying laundry flapping against fire escape rails.

Manhattan was New York's crown. Brooklyn was the city's heart and lungs.

The delis in Brooklyn's Williamsburg were distinctively perfumed by kosher dills bobbling in brine, and the scent of honey cake and challah. There were old red-checkered tablecloth Italian *jernts* in Red Hook serving spaghetti with garlicky red clam sauce and speckled bricks of spumoni. There were yeasty-scented Irish pubs in Flatbush, glowering and giddy, and spotless Scandinavian bakeries in Bay Ridge, sober and bright. Street stands in Canarsie sold long skinny salted pretzels and technicolored Italian ices, while men with handkerchief-hats fluffed over their bald heads clacked bocci balls and families sat on stoops below their open windows, Caruso, Sinatra, and Louis Prima crackling over record players out into the streets, as kids bickered over stoopball rules, played for stakes of lime rickeys, malted milks, and egg creams.

Manhattan boasted that the world came to its doorstep. But Brooklyn was at the Statue of Liberty's side door, and much of the world moved in. There were Italians, Irish, Poles, and Swedes, Germans in Bensonhurst, and blacks who had moved up from the South into Stuyvesant Heights. There were Russians in Greenpoint, some of New York's first Syrians and West Indians, and, most exotic of all, a community of Newfoundlanders, fishing families, who had come to settle in Prospect Park West.

More than a third of the borough's population was Jewish. In the mid-1940's, Brooklyn was probably the world's largest Jewish territory. Williamsburg, Bensonhurst, and Crown Heights abounded with Jews of every variation, from Orthodox to Reform, secular to Hasidic and Lubavitcher; from stoop-backed Talmudic scholars wrapped in teffilin to Murder Incorporated mobsters in shimmering sharkskin suits. Brooklyn Jews were considered La Guardia and Roosevelt lovers (both Franklin and Eleanor), *New York Post* and *PM* readers, and champions of Henry Wallace, the Hollywood Ten, Leon Trotsky, kibbutzniks, and fellow travelers. From Pistol Pete Reiser to Paul Robeson, Brooklyn loved lefties.

This figured in the thinking of Branch Rickey, who left the St. Louis Cardinals to become general manager of Brooklyn's baseball team in 1942. He had run the St. Louis Cardinals for nine years. Missouri was an old border state in which segregation was still observed, but Brooklyn was a different territory. White Brooklynites were not any more liberal than most white Alabamians when it came to welcoming blacks next door. But Branch Rickey believed that he might persuade Brooklyn Dodgers fans to accept an accomplished black athlete in the Brooklyn Dodgers infield.

All characterizations of a place as vast and varied as

Brooklyn were, of course, incomplete. In 1947, Brooklyn also had some avenues so elegant (still does) as to make Central Park West covetous. It had outposts of high culture, a dense and intense society, a cosmopolitan outlook, and—a last mark of a vital society—its own utterly distinct accent. Manhattan was "Rhapsody in Blue," bright lights, and DiMagg. Brooklyn was *dese, dose,* and *dem*— Dem Bums.

Only a team greatly loved could become known by so many nicknames. *Dodgers* itself was shortened from *Trolley Dodgers,** the sobriquet Manhattanites hung on all citizens of the borough across the East River. *Dem Bums* was the moniker meted out by a frustrated fan who sat in the grandstand seats just below the press box. Other fans and reporters picked up his bleats whenever Dodgers booted ground balls, threw to the wrong base, or—as they did at least once in a game against the Boston Braves in 1926—contrived to have three base runners arrive at third base at the same time. Who's on first? *Evvverybody!* The team was also called *the Flock,* from the days when they were managed by Wilbert Robinson, and his players

---

* There was a faint suggestion of criminal conduct in the phrase that may be less apparent today. Trolley dodgers were often those who ducked and evaded the front end of trolleys so they could latch onto the back end and ride for free.

were known as *the Robins*. Manhattan sports sections tended to boldface them as *the Brooks*.

The Dodgers, by any and all of their names, grew out of the Brooklyn baseball team that was created for the old American Association in 1884. They were determinedly un-Yankee-like from the first. The Dodgers cultivated working-class fans by playing their games on Sundays, the only full day off for many laborers. Ticket prices were cheap, so as to leave sufficient budget for beer, from which the team made its real money.

Brooklynites spoke of the team with an affection that was deepened by familiarity, identification, and accumulating frustration. Fans followed and admired the Yankees; they cheered for the Giants; they lived and died with the Dodgers. Ebbets Field was as flesh-and-blood familiar to most Brooklynites as their own block, their church, or their synagogue. The Dodgers were community property in a port of entry for immigrants and new arrivals. In a borough that often felt stunted and overshadowed by the towers of Manhattan, the Dodgers were an emblem of big-city status. As much as the Brooklyn Bridge, Ebbets Field was a gateway to an enchanted territory.

Yankee Stadium was as large and sumptuous as a great cathedral. But Ebbets Field, at 55 Sullivan Place flat smack in the middle of Flatbush, was small and close, *haimish*, as was said in the delis and shuls of Williamsburg. With just 32,000 seats, it held some of the same disordered warmth and jumble of an overstuffed family apartment. The first and third base foul lines were no farther from fans' seats than the length of an apartment house hallway. Yankee fans might be able to see Phil Rizzuto smile, but Dodger fans could see when Pee Wee Reese broke into a sweat. Clothier Abe Stark put up a signboard in right-center field:

HIT SIGN, WIN SUIT

Few did. (The fence in right center field, happily enough for Abe Stark, was the farthest from home plate at 403 feet; the left field foul post was fixed just 357 feet away—where a sign could have cost Mr. Stark a lot of haberdashery.)* But the implication was also important: while Yankee sluggers got tailored on Fifth Avenue, journeymen Dodgers slugged for Abe Stark's sign. There was a gap at the bottom of the metal gate in right center field, which was thoughtfully left unbreached, so Brooklyn kids could put their sweaters and chins carefully against the sidewalk and see the backsides of Carl Furillo and Eddie Stanky chase plays around the field. A brewery installed a neon sign atop the right-center scoreboard:

SCHAEFER

---

* As it was, he prospered and was elected Brooklyn borough president in 1960.

The H blinked to signify a hit; the E lit up when the scorer ruled an error. The Dodger Sym-phony, a five-piece band from Greenpoint, kept a chorus going in the left field bleachers through most home games, playing "Three Blind Mice" when the umpires took the field. The close quarters and familial kidding, the birthday cakes fans dropped off at the locker room for their favorite players, the players hanging on a passenger strap in a Brighton Beach train car on its way to Ebbets Field, riding the subway like any workman—all made the Dodgers part of Brooklyn's heartbeat.

The Dodgers reached the World Series in 1920; they lost to the Cleveland Indians. They finished fifth and sixth through the rest of the 1920s, then sank into last place during the 1930s. Those were the decades in which the team's character was instilled: winsome losers, adorable incompetents, perennial basement-dwellers buoyed by steadfast fans with pungent accents. Westbrook Pegler, the best-read columnist of the time, dubbed them "The Daffiness Boys."

Baseball clubs seeking tax breaks from their communities like to point out that sports teams are also cultural institutions. By the 1940s, the Brooklyn Dodgers were more of a cultural institution than a competitive baseball team.

The team was revitalized in 1939 when an operator named Larry McPhail came to town from Cincinnati to run the club. They played the first of their World Series against the New York Yankees in 1941, and were about to win the fourth game to tie the Yankees at two apiece when Hugh Casey threw a strikeout curve to Tommy Heinrich. But the spin of the curve was so strong—or, as some Brooklyn fans might have it, the fates were so fixed—that the ball slipped through the web of the glove of catcher Mickey Owen and dribbled toward the backstop, guided by a force no more visible than that which steers a candy wrapper across a street. Owen, a shrewd and experienced catcher, began to turn as soon as he felt the ball was missing from his mitt. But his path to the ball was blocked, by blue-suited New York cops with their backs turned to keep Dodger fans from rushing the field in celebration. Heinrich took first base. The Yankees scored four runs to win that game, and then won the next one, to win the World Series. Brooklyn had just begun to mend its crushed heart two months later, when Pearl Harbor was bombed.

Half a century after they left Flatbush for Los Angeles, the Brooklyn Dodgers are still among the best-known sports franchises in history. The name of a team so profitably departed is probably still better known than that of most teams that have come into baseball by expansion over the past generation. The players, arrayed in loose-fitting flannels with a cursive *Brooklyn* rolling over their chests like the interlacing lines on a subway map; the fans, in an immense community of diverse clans and villages; and the ways in which the fans found themselves reflected in the players, the field, and even the feeling that their striving often went overlooked and unrewarded, all amounted to absolute empathy.

We can still treat ourselves to a reverie of Brooklyn on a summer's night: front room windows lifted open up and down the broad avenues, Atlantic, Neptune, and Flatlands; bikes at rest against candy stores; men in beach chairs replanted in front of cigar stores, women in flowered housedresses watching kids clamber over brownstone stoops on small, tight streets; the rumble of the BMT against your toes; the overhead iron clangor of the elevated train prickling your ears; the aroma of the Taystee Bread bakery perfuming the walk over from Prospect Park Station; and the magnolia-scented voice of Red Barber coming in over the radio from Ebbets Field (in Brooklyn, after all, Mississippians were just another group of immigrants) softly suffusing the night, giving the streets the feel of a front porch. Preacher on the mound, Pee Wee patrolling short, Robbie just beside him, and Hilda Chester of Flatbush swinging a cowbell between pitches. *Dem Bums.* That team, in that neighborhood, seemed exactly what a national game is *supposed* to be.

4

Barred in Boston

I t seems clearer now than it could have in 1945 that official segregation was a ruined and doomed institution. Racial segregation was immoral, corrupt, inefficient, and undermined by its own contradictions. The United States could not have won World War II, or beaten back the Great Depression of the 1930s, without black workers in its factories, fields, and armed services. Just as Britain had discovered that it could not win a war for freedom and keep an empire, the United States was learning that it could not be considered the last, best hope for mankind while enchaining its own citizens with race laws.

The complexion of power in America was changing, especially in its major cities. Blacks had become significant, if mostly still separate, economic, cultural, and political factors in New York, Chicago, Philadelphia, Detroit, Boston, and Cleveland. The time segregation was taking to wind down would still damage many lives, but the fuel segregation needed to burn was running low. The generation that had won a world war was the last that would live by segregation; they would, in fact, abolish it.

Perhaps organized sports became the first great public test of segregation because fairness is fundamental in competitive games. "Separate but equal" seemed particularly ludicrous when applied to an enterprise in which the whole point was excellence tested by competition.

The range of editorial support for the integration of major league baseball was wide. It had been gathering for ten years. It ranged from the left, on the sports pages of the Communist Party's *Daily Worker* (the most distinguished section of the newspaper—if only the paper had been as lucid about Joseph Stalin as it was about Joe DiMaggio), to Westbrook Pegler on the right (and if he had only been as lucid about Joseph McCarthy).

The black press, most notably Sam Lacy of the *Baltimore Afro-American* and Wendell Smith of the *Pittsburgh Courier*, were not only outspoken but inventive in devising ways to keep the question of baseball's integration a continuing news story (Wendell Smith polled Southern-born major league players on the question; the surprising result was that most said they would accept black teammates). Shirley Povich of the *Washington Post*, the most esteemed sports columnist in the nation's capital—still a segregated capital—forcefully supported letting blacks into major league baseball. So did many of the nation's leading celebrity columnists, including Damon Runyon and Ed Sullivan. Consequently, by the close of World War II the rationale for continued racial segregation of the national game—and, perhaps, all race laws—had been subtly but substantially changed. Segregation was rarely defended as being right, only that it *was*.

Baseball commissioner Kenesaw Landis maintained that no rule prohibited blacks from playing major league baseball. Black players themselves, he said with a straight face, were simply too successful in the Negro Leagues to want to play in the majors. (I wonder if any reporter ever challenged him to name even one black player who had told him that.)* Or, said the commissioner, white Southern players (who had been eager to play against black stars, especially Satchel Paige, in profitable exhibition games) would not accept black players in their own uniforms.

In fact, major league baseball had an investment to

---

* Of course, the argument was nonsense. But it touched on what would become one of the unintended consequences of baseball's integration—a number of white players would lose their jobs to more talented black ballplayers. But integration would also mean the downfall of the Negro Leagues, costing the jobs of black ballplayers who could not find places in the major leagues.

protect, and that investment was in segregation. Many clubs rented their ballparks when they traveled to Negro League teams. The Yankees, White Sox, and Washington Senators, for example, commonly earned more than $100,000 a year by hiring out Yankee Stadium, Comiskey Park, and Griffith Stadium for Negro League games. It was a steady, almost leisurely source of income that major league owners wanted to keep.

The commissioner said that any major league team that wanted to sign a black player would be permitted to do so; they would have his support. But he knew of no black player who wanted to forego his own comfortable Negro League career (grueling long-distance bus rides, malevolent local sheriffs, shabby hotels, and crooked promoters chiseling gate receipts) to play in the major leagues. Everyone, black, white, and Latino, was prosperous and content in a league of his own.

That tranquil assurance had been tested, however, early in 1945, by a man whose name is not found in most sports histories: Isadore Muchnick. Muchnick was a Boston city councillor, not a baseball man. He represented Roxbury, whose constituency was then becoming a definitive Eleanor Roosevelt–loving demographic mix of liberal Jews and blacks.

Boston had blue laws. Sunday baseball was permitted, but only because the city council ruled that it was not mere entertainment or diversion, but some kind of civic institution (a civic institution, to be sure, that sold beer). As World War II wound down, Muchnick declared that he would move to deprive Boston's two major league baseball teams of this dispensation unless both the Red Sox and Braves gave tryouts to black ballplayers. Eddie Collins, the general manager of the Red Sox, contacted Muchnick to say they would be delighted to sign a black athlete, but no black ballplayer was willing to leave the Negro Leagues for the chance of a major league career.

Isadore Muchnick made the note public; within days, he heard from Wendell Smith. Smith told him that, on the contrary, any and all Negro League players would welcome the chance to bring their talents to the attention of the Boston Red Sox. More to the point, he offered to deliver a few. Muchnick conveyed this news to Eddie Collins. The Red Sox general manager was stuck. Collins said that *if* Wendell Smith could deliver three players willing to undergo tryouts—and *if* his newspaper, not the club, would pay their way to Boston—and *if* it was understood that no spots on the team were actually available—Red Sox management would be willing to look them over. Short of promising to sing "Mammy," it is hard to construct a more patronizing invitation.

But Wendell Smith was a gracious and practical man. He accepted the Red Sox offer. Either conceivable result held the prospect of a good story. Smith was certain that he could deliver players whose athletic skills and promise would tempt the Red Sox to change their policies—or finally confirm, for any who could still harbor doubts, that major league baseball was segregated. Teams like the Red Sox (perhaps especially the Red Sox, who would not integrate until Pumpsie Green was signed in 1959) preferred losing games to desegregating the national pastime.

So on April 16, 1945, the day after Franklin D. Roosevelt was buried, and just as Soviet troops drove into Berlin, Wendell Smith presented three Negro League players in Fenway whom he considered so gifted as to make the major leagues wince at what they had willingly overlooked. Sam Jethroe of the Cleveland Buckeyes was twenty-seven. Marvin Williams of the Philadelphia Stars was just twenty. And Jack Roosevelt Robinson of the Kansas City Monarchs was twenty-six.

Contemporary press accounts of the morning are incomplete. There were about fifty other walk-ons, stretching and squatting on the field, high school or sandlot players, all of them overseen by seventy-eight-year-old Hugh Duffy, a Boston scout. Hugh Duffy's presence was probably a sign of the inconsequence of the tryout—scouts have no executive authority. The Red Sox were opening their season the next day in New York. Their roster was set. The proceedings were useful only for any possible value they had as physical exercise. Shoeless Joe Hardy could have shown up, thundering home runs, singing and dancing, and not have cracked the Boston lineup on that day.

But all accounts agree: the three Negro League players showed promise. And Jackie Robinson, the most experienced, was superb. He slashed long line drives off of Fenway's looming left field wall, clanking the numbered tin plates in the scoreboard.

"Bang. Bang. Bang. He *rattled* it," Isadore Muchnick told the *Boston Globe* in 1959. He remembers going up to Boston manager Joe Cronin, who had been watching from the dugout for a few minutes, his attention perhaps drawn by Robinson's ringing of the left field wall. "He said to me," remembered Muchnick, "'if we had that guy on our club, we'd be a world-beater.'" Wendell Smith remembered Hugh Duffy shaking his head with a smile after Robinson delicately guided a few bunts down the baselines. Robinson's virtuoso versatility was apparent: he could hit the ball long, and he could steer it short. "What a ballplayer!" said old Hugh Duffy. "Too bad he's the wrong color."

The three Negro League stars then filled out forms, had sandwiches at the Boston train terminal, kidded one another about their performances, and departed for their separate trains back to Cleveland, Kansas City, and Philadelphia, to play against one another for the rest of the year. None of them ever heard from the Boston Red Sox again. Sam Jethroe says, "We knew they were just doing it to please the councilman. We knew nothing would come of it." Rachel Robinson, who was then finishing nursing school in Southern California, says that

49

Jackie scarcely mentioned the morning to her. Former Lieutenant Robinson had learned about flanking maneuvers in army tank exercises.

Boston was an outstanding team with a conspicuous weakness. Their great, aging first baseman, Jimmie Foxx, had been traded and retired during World War II. While Bobby Doerr at second and Johnny Pesky at shortstop were among the premier infielders in the league, the Red Sox needed help at a particular spot. Jackie Robinson was a more accomplished, experienced, and better-known athlete than any among Boston's minor league clubs. And more: Jackie Robinson knew how to win—football games, courts-martial, and games playing behind Satchel Paige. It is hard to suppose that a manager could have seen Jackie Robinson stripping Fenway's left field wall with line drives on that day and not wondered how he would look wearing a first baseman's glove.*

Yet Joe Cronin, who would eventually become president of the American League, told reporters before his death in 1984 that signing Jackie Robinson (or Jethroe or Williams) was simply impossible for Boston to contemplate. The Red Sox AAA affiliate was Louisville. Ken-

---

* As it was, the Red Sox would use five men at first base over the next five years before settling on Walt Dropo.

tucky was not Quebec, where Jackie Robinson would soon be sent by the Dodgers to play for Montreal. Of course, if Boston had been authentically interested in Robinson, there were other avenues. They might have sent him to a lower minor league affiliate for a year, or induced him to play with several Red Sox stars in a winter league in Latin America, where he could become seasoned for the challenge to come.

But the tryouts were authentic only as a political gesture. They were meant to mollify a few politicians, sportswriters, clergy, and editorialists. Boston was just about as interested in signing Jackie Robinson as it was in a return of the Tea Tax.

Even then, the Boston Red Sox were notoriously bedeviled by the Yankees. They had finished second to New York in 1938, 1939, 1941, and 1942, before the massive mobilization of World War II scattered major league players. The Red Sox were replenished by the postwar return of Ted Williams and Dom DiMaggio. They won the American League pennant in 1946. Sending Robinson, Jethroe, and Williams away from Fenway in the spring of 1945 might have looked reasonable then—for one season. But the club slipped to third in 1947, behind New York and Detroit; rallied to take second place in 1948, just a game behind the Cleveland Indians; and finished just a game out of first in 1949, once again behind the

Yankees. Year after year—after year—Boston seemed to fall just a player short.*

It is irresistible to imagine how their prospects might have improved if the player they had chosen to add had been Jackie Robinson. Imagine Robinson getting on base, dancing beyond the bag, daunting and rattling a pitcher to set the stage for Ted Williams: For decades, Red Sox fans have laughingly rationalized their losses with the thought that they were an unwarranted curse, inflicted for selling Babe Ruth to the New York Yankees. But I've come to see their hardships after 1945 as a blight they brought down on themselves. Boston barred the door to Jackie Robinson in the spring of 1945, when the team and the city had an exceptional, indispensable chance to advance themselves and enrich the country.

---

* Sam Jethroe would eventually be signed by Branch Rickey in Brooklyn, play for Montreal, and get traded to the Boston Braves. He was the National League Rookie of the Year in 1950. Marvin Williams would play in the Texas League, but never major league baseball.

5

Mr. Rickey's Little List

M ost major league clubs had regarded the years of World War II as a state of suspended animation. They would sign such retired and retread players as they needed to field a team. But no title won during that time would be taken seriously. The teams they deployed, while containing many worthy, hard-working men getting their one chance at major league recognition, were semipro barnstormers borrowing big league livery. Real competition would not resume until the war was won and all the best players had returned home.

When Branch Wesley Rickey came from St. Louis to take charge of the Brooklyn Dodgers, the sturdiest part of his reputation was as the innovator who had devised baseball's system of farm clubs. Brooklyn, with its smaller fan base and financial resources, despaired of finding and outbidding the Yankees and Giants for young talent. Rickey had created a kind of model in St. Louis for finding able young men in overlooked hollers and street corners, signing them as boys, assigning them to farm clubs, and making them major leaguers before the Yankees, Red Sox, or Tigers knew what they had missed.

Rickey came to the board of the Brooklyn Trust, the bank that held the largest share of the Dodgers, early in the 1942 season with a brash suggestion. Most teams had essentially folded their scouting operations during the war. You did not need scouts to find old pros and one-armed outfielders scattered around the country to fill out a team. It was assumed that few people playing during this period were worth appraising for the future; otherwise, they would be serving their country.

But Rickey told the bankers that he wanted to expand Brooklyn's scouting program. He had an interest in the wider world beyond baseball (he professed to discipline himself to read the front section of the morning newspaper before turning to sports), which had convinced him that the United States was in for a long war. Players who were, say, seventeen on the morning that Pearl Harbor was bombed could be twenty or twenty-one by the time Mussolini, Hitler, and Tojo were routed. Rickey proposed deploying scouts to uncover promising young players who could be in place when the war ended.

Brooklyn, he told the bankers, could essentially skim the cream of a whole new generation of baseball talent. The bankers liked the sound of that. Perhaps they also liked the cost. In those days, scouts cost a team only modest wages and occasional phone calls.

With the premise of his scheme accepted, Rickey moved to broaden its reach. Some of the best players in overlooked places, he said, were in Latin America. Rickey suggested sending scouts there, too. The bankers agreed; scouting costs were even lower in Mexico, Puerto Rico, the Dominican Republic, Venezuela, Panama, and Cuba. A number of American-born players could be found on teams there. But, Rickey continued, many of the finest young talents were to be found among Latin players themselves.* Or, he said almost casually, black American baseball players supplementing their Negro League salaries by playing in Latin America. The bankers did not flinch. "So I would also propose," he said finally, "also sending some of our scouts to Negro League games to see what's there."

"Why not?" Rickey remembered the bankers muttering around a rosewood table. "You might find something good." By keeping major league baseball exclusively

---

* A few Cubans and Florida-born Cuban-Americans had already played for major and minor league teams. Al Lopez had broken in with Brooklyn in 1928. The player's ancestry was usually cautiously advertised as Spanish, not Latin.

white for the entire century, baseball men had essentially invested in segregation. Perhaps it took bankers, who knew that the characteristics of America were changing, to say, "Why not?"

By the time Jackie Robinson had been turned away by the Boston Red Sox, he had already been identified to Branch Rickey as the leading candidate to break baseball's color barrier.*

Earlier in April, Rickey had given a tryout of his own to two Negro League players, Terris McDuffie of the Newark Eagles and Dave "Showboat" Thomas of the New York Cubans, but grudgingly. Joe Bostic of the *Harlem People's Voice,* a Communist newspaper, had engineered the tryout at the Dodgers' training facility in the Catskills. Mr. Rickey distrusted Communists (about Yalta and Berlin as much as baseball), and thought that the two players Bostic brought along must have been unswerving

---

*As Robinson himself always acknowledged, he was not the first African American in major league baseball. Black players, while not numerous, had appeared through the 1880s. Brothers Fleet and Welday Walker of Toledo were probably the most prominent. The prohibition against blacks was passed in 1887 at the behest of Cap Anson of the Chicago White Stockings, the game's most powerful player and team operator. Of course, it is also only realistic to assume that even after 1887, a number of major league players born in the Old South had black ancestors, if unacknowledged.

socialists because, according to Rickey's reports, they could not hit a curve ball.*

Rickey also held a low opinion of the Negro Leagues—not the ballplayers, but the owners and operators. Rickey considered most of the Negro League franchises to be undisciplined, unprofessional, and underhanded about contracts, commitments, and pay. He knew that many Negro League teams earned as much revenue through gambling as through gate receipts. He regarded the clubs as floating crap games that used baseballs—as exhibitionist as fan dancing, as exploitative as bordellos.

(And in this opinion he had an outspoken ally in Jackie Robinson.)

After those tryouts, Rickey had announced that he was creating a Brooklyn Brown Dodgers baseball club to compete in the new United States League being formed by Gus Greenlee, the owner of the Pittsburgh Crawfords Negro League team. There is little to suggest that Rickey planned to actually field such a team (if major league baseball had refused to accept black players—perhaps). The Brown Dodgers were a phantom franchise that Rickey concocted in a press release. It effectively concealed the assignment of Brooklyn's top scouts as they went to Negro League games and openly approached the

---

* Neither McDuffie nor Thomas ever went on to play in the major leagues.

players whose names had been passed on to Branch Rickey as candidates to break baseball's racial barrier.*

It is worth reviewing some of those names, if only to remind us how wrong contemporary press accounts and histories can be.

There is no evidence that Branch Rickey and his scouts ever seriously considered the best-known Negro League players of the day. The first hindrance many had was simply age. Martin Dihigo, the Cuban-born star who may have been the most versatile pure baseball talent ever to play the game (he not only played every position on the field, from pitcher to catcher, but excelled at all of them), was already forty.[†] Josh Gibson of the Homestead Grays, who may have been the most prodigious home run hitter of all time (he would routinely hit between 50 and 75 home runs a year, many of them Ruthian—or Gibsonian), was just thirty-four. But he was already afflicted with the

---

* The league never came about. Gus Greenlee was only slightly more serious in his intentions than Branch Rickey. With contracts being so casual in the Negro Leagues, Greenlee had mostly hoped to sign some of the biggest stars for the Crawfords. At any rate, the integration of major league baseball proceeded so quickly that the Negro Leagues were effectively closed by 1950.
† Dihigo, who surely deserves a book, movie, ballet, and musical comedy about his life, ended his playing career in Cuba and became Fidel Castro's minister of sports. As near as I can tell, he is the only man to be a member of the Cuban, Mexican, and U.S. National Baseball Halls of Fame.

emotional problems and alcoholism that would claim his life by 1947. Gibson's teammate Buck Leonard, known for striking lacerating line drives, was thirty-eight. (In 1937, Washington Senators owner Clark Griffith had summoned Gibson and Leonard to his office to ask if they were willing to play for the Senators. They were. But then Griffith, not Gibson and Leonard, lost his nerve.)*

And then, of course, there was Satchel Paige of the Kansas City Monarchs. It is always worth lingering over his name.

How old was Satchel Paige as Branch Rickey pondered his choice in the closing days of World War II? He was at least thirty-eight; more likely forty; then again, possibly forty-three. Rickey was less discouraged about Paige's chronological age than about the age in his arm. Satchel Paige had pitched virtually every day for a quarter of a century. He had pitched on searing summer days in Kansas City, on bone-cold prairie nights during exhibitions in Edmonton, and on blistering February afternoons barnstorming in Santo Domingo. Paige pitched at least three innings every day so promoters could guarantee paying customers that any kind of ticket bought them a look at the great Satchel Paige. How many pitches could possibly be left in his wiry arm and wily mind?

---

* Today, both Gibson and Leonard are in the Hall of Fame.

Rickey believed that Paige was more of a stage performer than a baseball player. And yet, to sign him
would be to own the biggest box office attraction in
baseball. The Dodgers would have a hurler who had left
Babe Ruth, Joe DiMaggio, and Ted Williams screwing
themselves into the back line of the batter's box after
swinging at his pitches, and been acclaimed by Dizzy
Dean as the outright best pitcher in history. He was not a
man who would shrink from the challenge Rickey had in
mind, or wilt under all the attention and tension.

Satchel Paige was his own man. He was also, alas, his
own manager. He disdained physical exercise, temporal
authority, marital vows, tax laws, and baseball rules.
Paige's personality could be sparkling. And that was
exactly what alarmed the Dodgers. He enjoyed enter-
taining (and that would seem to be the word) reporters
with accounts of his high life, and high jinks.

Satchel Paige was one of the best acts in America.
Porters would invent bogus breakdowns to hold trains
for him, waiting twenty, thirty minutes, sluicing steam
onto the platform, until at last Paige would stride out
into the haze with unhurried elegance, his custom-
finished cuffs flashing gold, hailing the porters and his
teammates, "Gentlemen, let us ramble!" He reminded
scouts that he, Satchel Paige, not Joe DiMaggio or Ted
Williams, was already the highest-paid baseball player in
the United States. Why would he want to take a pay cut
to play for a white man? It would be like asking Duke

Ellington if he wanted to take a second-chair spot with the New York Philharmonic.

And yet, if they would only ask, Paige was willing. The chance to finally confirm his mastery in the major leagues was worth financial sacrifice. Breaking major league baseball's color barrier would be the final sign that Satchel Paige had made the powers of baseball meet his terms. But Rickey was disinclined. Questions about Paige's age and proclivity for naughtiness gave way to a caution: pitchers threw beanballs. They had to. The threat of mutual retaliation helped define the confrontation between pitchers and hitters. Rickey did not see Satchel Paige heeding his entreaties to pass by the opportunity to brush a pitch close to an opponent's chin. The hallowed baseball custom of a pitcher backing a player away from the plate could touch off a riot, he feared, if the pitcher was black and the hitter was white. So Satchel Paige, at an early stage, was excluded from Rickey's consideration.*

---

* Happily, all of Rickey's reservations would soon be proved groundless. Bill Veeck signed Satchel Paige for the Cleveland Indians for the 1948 season. Paige proved that he could still be, for an inning or two, the best pitcher in baseball. He helped Cleveland win the World Series and, at the age of forty plus, was selected the American League Rookie of the Year, an honor he declined with more dignity than was deserved. Rickey brought pitcher Don Newcomb onto the Brooklyn squad in 1949. He went on to win both the Cy Young and Most Valuable Player awards in 1956, and threw the more-than-occasional beanball without incident.

Ray Dandridge, the velvet-gloved third baseman, was thirty-two, closer to the age Rickey had in mind. But Dandridge had spent World War II playing baseball in Mexico (rather than serving the country in which he was excluded in many states from using a public toilet, much less playing major league baseball). Rickey preferred the publicity value of a veteran.* Ironically, army service was exactly what kept Monte Irvin of the Newark Eagles from being considered. Before World War II, Irvin was often regarded as the young Negro Leaguer with the best chance of being signed for the majors. Like Jackie Robinson, he was a four-sport college athlete; he was a Negro Leagues batting champion while Jackie Robinson was still in college, and an exceptionally articulate man. But as Branch Rickey reviewed scouting reports in the spring and summer of 1945, Monte Irvin was still with the Army Engineers in occupied Germany—where Jackie Robinson would have been on duty had not his acquittal in a court-martial hastened his departure from the U.S. Army.†

In the end, Rickey lingered over several names. But brooding always led him back to Jackie Robinson. Rickey

---

* Dandridge would eventually be signed by the Giants organization and become the Pacific Coast League's Most Valuable Player with the AAA Minneapolis Millers. He is also in the Baseball Hall of Fame.
† Monte Irvin would be signed by the New York Giants in 1950, playing for the Giants, Cubs, and, very briefly, with the minor league Los Angeles Angels before retiring. He became an assistant to the commissioner of baseball in 1968, and was elected to the Hall of Fame.

was greatly charmed by Roy Campanella, a twenty-four-year-old catcher (whose mixed Italian-African-American ancestry could be a hot ticket in Brooklyn). But Campanella was an ebullient man who enjoyed card games, good times, and carousing—he was a ballplayer. Rickey would soon sign him for the Dodger organization. But he did not want Campanella to suffer the kind of unforgiving scrutiny the first black Dodger would have to withstand from the press.* Don Newcomb of the Newark Eagles was also clearly superior. But Newcomb was just nineteen years old, and a pitcher, which gave the same caution to his selection as it did for Paige.

Yet the reasoning that finally led to the choice of Jackie Robinson (and Robinson alone; Rickey's first instinct had been to sign three black players at the same time) was not a process of elimination. Robinson was a complete and polished package. He could run, hit, hit with power, and field with grace. He could steal bases and bunt shrewdly, and he excelled in the game's mental aspects. He was a college man, a veteran, a world-caliber athlete, and a dark, handsome, round-shouldered man with a shy smile.

Rickey was encouraged by another fact. Robinson had played with and against white people all his life: as a

----

* Campanella, of course, would win the National League Most Valuable Player Award three times before a car crash smashed his legs and ended his career. Reporters, it must be noted, treasured him—and even found his gregarious ways an invigorating contrast to Jackie Robinson's rectitude.

child in Pasadena, as a young man at UCLA (in fact, the U.S. Army and the Kansas City Monarchs were the only times that Robinson had lived in segregated circumstances). He was not awed by white people, or irritated by them. Playing sports at UCLA had saturated him with a spotlight that exceeded the kind of attention that any Negro League player, save for Satchel Paige, had ever withstood.

Rickey had made careful inquiries about Robinson's personal life. He learned that he had been born in rural Cairo, Georgia, January 31, 1919, but was brought out to sunlit Southern California as an infant. He never really knew his father, Jerry, who left the family of five to run after another man's wife shortly after Jack Roosevelt (for Teddy) was born. His mother, Mallie, was a smart, devout, determined woman who worked as a domestic. The Robinsons were Methodists. The family lived on the other side of the tracks—or, as it often was in Southern California, the highway—of one of the most glamorous cities in America. The blacks, Mexicans, Asians, and Southern whites who were the Robinsons' neighbors on Pepper Street cleaned the mansions of movie people, tended their pools and gardens, and cared for their cars. But most of them could not see movies at the Pasadena Playhouse, or swim in the Pasadena Community Center Pool. Jackie Robinson would grow up to star in Pasadena's Rose Bowl.

Jackie's remarkable athletic skills were recognized

from the time he was seven or eight and older kids gave him part of their school lunches to play on their teams. He picked up a Ping-Pong paddle at a local YMCA one afternoon when he was fifteen; he thought it was a stupid-looking implement, apt for a silly game. Within a few months, he won the Pasadena city Ping-Pong championships—the first time his name appeared in a newspaper.

Jackie Robinson had done some running with a high-spirited crowd as a teenager. He was arrested a couple of times—for speeding, for disorderly conduct; if the crowd had been white, the police might have ignored them. But there was always a high school coach to approach the police with an apology and a promise that young Jack would avoid future infractions. When his older brother Frank was killed in a motorcycle accident, Jackie's absorption with sports seemed to sharpen. He told a few friends that he felt he was playing for Frank.

He won an athletic scholarship to Pasadena City College. One afternoon, Robinson set a record for the long jump at a meet in Pomona, leapt into a car to be driven to a baseball game in Glendale, arrived in the third inning, got two hits, stole two bases, and won the game for Pasadena. Jackie Robinson was offered scholarships around the country. He chose UCLA to stay close to his family. Jackie Robinson, it was said, was a bit of a mama's boy.

Robinson was engaged to marry a nurse. He did not drink, smoke, or fool around.

The one note in his biography that gave Brooklyn scouts any pause about Jackie Robinson was his court-martial. They knew that to be "honorably relieved from active duty" signified at least a small disagreement with the army. When Rickey learned that the spark of the dispute was Lieutenant Robinson's refusal to move to the back of a bus in a small, isolated town in the middle of Texas, he was delighted. The other names brought to his attention belonged to exceptional athletes (it is remarkable how many wound up in the Hall of Fame); many of them were accomplished, and even noble. But in Jackie Robinson, Branch Rickey thought he recognized the qualities of a man eager to ride forward—a knight. He told his chief scout, Clyde Sukeforth, "I think it is time for me to meet Mr. Robinson."

Sukeforth was almost more impressed by the following phrase, which he had never heard from Branch Rickey, a man who made it his business to meet with bankers, mayors, baseball commissioners, and the occasional mob boss; he would never hear it again:

"And if he can't get away to meet me," he told Clyde Sukeforth, "I am willing to go anywhere to meet him."

6

"Oh, What a Pair, Those Two!"

I t is not too strong to say that we are speaking of a kind of love. Branch Rickey, who was sensitive to any smack of patronizing Robinson, had always characterized the close relationship the two men seemed to develop at once as filial, not paternal. But Robinson himself, who was utterly secure in his certainty that no one could patronize Jackie Robinson, did not shy away from saying that Branch Rickey became a father to him, for Robinson had grown up without a father in his life.

Branch Rickey Jr., who ran the Dodgers' minor league operations, said that he had sensed a shared identity between the two that was as close as father and son, comfortably unruffled by the kinds of resentments and rivalries that can irritate families. In fact, Rickey Jr. would be this blunt: "I always knew that my father had a second son in Jackie."

Robinson would go on to play for other general managers. None defended him as fiercely as Branch Rickey, or took such unselfish delight in his excellence. Rickey oversaw scores of other players, and hundreds more on his minor league teams. None would be so closely wound into his own life as Robinson.

No doubt something exceptional flashed between the sixty-four-year-old beetle-browed baseball oligarch and the twenty-six-year-old rookie Negro League shortstop. After just their first two hours of conversation in front of the fish tank that bubbled in Rickey's corner office, Branch Rickey was emboldened to rely on Robinson alone as his knight to break baseball's color barrier. And Jackie Robinson was persuaded to rein in the combativeness that fueled his competitive fires.

By the summer of 1945, Rickey had a rising sense of urgency. No other teams were preparing to sign blacks.* But events were threatening to overtake his planning,

---

* Bill Veeck was prevented from purchasing the Philadelphia Phillies largely because he had planned to do exactly that. But although he had bought the Cleveland Indians by 1947, he did not bring Newark Eagle star Larry Doby onto the team until three months after Jackie Robinson had debuted with Brooklyn.

which would deprive the Dodgers of their unrivaled entrée to the best players in the Negro Leagues, and Rickey of his place in history.

Following a series of riots in Harlem in 1943, Mayor Fiorello La Guardia had established a commission on discrimination and attacked both the symbolism and reality of baseball's segregation. He said he could not goad New York's stores, factories, and labor unions to open up to black workers while condoning job discrimination on the Yankees, Giants, and Dodgers. Rickey, who as far as he disclosed any political identity, seemed to be a liberal (Lincoln/La Guardia) Republican, agreed. He gave the mayor his personal if imprecise assurance that he was setting a course to break up the game's segregation.

The legal threat posed by La Guardia's persistence was minor league. At most, the mayor might have persuaded the city council to ban beer sales. And at the least, the major league clubs could have gone through the motions of a few more tryouts. But mayoral elections were approaching in November. La Guardia was retiring, and wanted to secure his legacy. Fiorello La Guardia was as fervent a performer on his field of play as—well, as Jackie Robinson. Rickey feared that the mayor's ardor to integrate New York's major league baseball teams might quickly propel the Giants along the same lines. Or make it appear as if the Dodgers' deliberate program to integrate had been inspired by—no, worse, *forced* by—Fiorello La Guardia. The man sportswriters referred to as "the Mahatma" was not going to be outshone on baseball integration by a mere mayor.

Branch Rickey was called the Mahatma because he seemed to toss out Gandhian bromides—"Luck is the residue of design," most famously, as well as, "Skill puts the chrome on courage," and, "Never play checkers with a man who carries his own board."

(Mohandas Gandhi, in fact, was not nearly so pithy and certain.)

Some sports figures seemed rarely to talk about anything weighty. Branch Rickey could make the decision about whether to bring in a right- or left-handed pitcher to face Stan Musial in the eighth inning sound like a deliberation over supporting Chiang Kai-shek or Mao Zedong. He could give baseball minutiae the same weight as matters of state—which could lend him an appearance of ridiculousness.

His appearance was easily lampooned—a diving bell silhouette, wooly mammoth eyebrows, Churchillian bow tie and swaggering cigar, a fedora raked back with FDR insouciance. Rickey was a lawyer by training and could martial magnificent courtroom elocutionary technique to convince a player that it was in his own interest not to insist on a raise.

"No man who ever played for me suffered educationally or morally," he used to observe. "If he wanted to continue in school, I helped him. And when his playing days were over, he had learned the lessons of clean living and moral stamina." Rickey believed that financial sacrifice was a virtue. "The most dangerous moral hazard in the field of professional sports," he used to lecture, "is leisure. Men are employed for only four hours out of twenty-four. The use of surplus funds and hours in the hands of very young men is a hazard. 'Nothing to do,' and too many means with which to do it is the most damnable thing that can come to a youth."

"Mr. Rickey has a heart of gold," one of his old players, Gene Hermanski, once said. "And he keeps it."

Rickey rather liked being hailed as the Mahatma, who was then enigmatic to many Americans, but nevertheless one of the most admired people on the planet. Rickey was less charmed by another news column nickname that seemed suggested by the flourish of his cigar: "El Cheapo." Another of Rickey's favorite players, Eddie Stanky, said of his contract negotiations, "I get a million dollars' worth of free advice and a very small raise."

The Mahatma kept a portrait of the Great Emancipator in his office, next to one of Leo Durocher (the Railsplitter alongside The Lip). Reporters often tried to read significance into his choice of office decoration. But sometimes a framed Lincoln is just a framed Lincoln. When Rickey was born in Stockdale, Ohio, in 1881,

Lincoln had been dead for only sixteen years. Branch Rickey grew up around people who remembered Lincoln's funeral train trolling slowly through southern Ohio's rolling fields on the way to deliver Lincoln back home to the soil of Illinois. Any Midwestern boy of Rickey's generation and intelligence would be tempted to take inspiration from Lincoln's legacy.

Some of Rickey's skeptics thought his agenda to integrate baseball was propelled by a desire to foster a profile that resembled Lincoln's. What would those skeptics have said if Rickey had kept that portrait of Lincoln brooding in his office, and then never tried to integrate baseball?

Rickey, for his part, assiduously refused any attempt to portray him as some kind of civil rights crusader. "All I did," he said time after time, "was pay a superbly talented athlete to play for Brooklyn and help us win a championship." But Jackie Robinson, a proud and outspoken man, did not feel diminished in putting Branch Rickey's bravery alongside his own.

It was often pointed out that Rickey had displayed no discernible interest in overturning baseball's color barrier when he ran the St. Louis Cardinals. He described Missouri as "stony soil" on that issue, a state in which public events, baseball included, still had segregated seating, a circumstance that Rickey never tried to change. Lincoln was not Lincoln all at once, either.

There was a story Rickey liked to tell, which to some smacked too calculatedly of young Abe Lincoln recalling the first time he saw slaves chained on the deck of a Mississippi riverboat. Around 1946, Rickey seemed suddenly to remember that when he had coached the Ohio Wesleyan College baseball team, he had a black player on the squad named Charles Thomas. Ohio Wesleyan went to South Bend, Indiana, to play Notre Dame, and wired ahead to their accustomed hotel for the required number of rooms. But when the desk clerk observed that a black man would occupy one of the rooms, he informed Rickey that the hotel did not admit blacks.

Rickey was outraged—and defiant. He directed the team's student manager to ring up the YMCA. But the YMCA, at least in South Bend, was no more accommodating than the hotel. At some point, Rickey's team needed to sleep. He checked in all of his players and staff, save for Charles Thomas, and had the hotel deliver a cot to his own room. The hotel balked; a desk clerk wouldn't have to be Alan Pinkerton to surmise that the cot was intended for Charles Thomas. But Rickey persisted, and suggested that the hotel's status as host for traveling college teams was at risk. Quietly, Charlie Thomas shared Branch Rickey's room.

That anecdote could stand alone as a pointed parable showing how conviction can sometimes outpoint bigotry. But when Rickey related the story, he added an epilogue. He said he returned to his room to find Charles Thomas sitting up on his cot, blinking back tears and rubbing the skin on the back of his hands.

"His huge, strong hands," Rickey would gravely declare, "rubbing themselves over and over in one another, as if he was trying to wring out their color. 'Black skin,'" Rickey said he heard Thomas muttering, "'*damned* black skin. If only I could make it white!'"

Reporters, almost reflexively, doubted the story. (No one had heard Rickey tell it before spring training in 1946.) But Charles Thomas was easily found. He had become a successful dentist in Albuquerque, New Mexico, and confirmed the story with more or less those same details. Rickey was pleased to instruct reporters that they were so intent in trying to chip away at his recollection that they had missed the whole point:

"Whatever impression that the episode left on Charlie Thomas," he told them, "it left a bigger impression on *me*."

By August 1945, chief scout Clyde Sukeforth had essentially been detailed to handle the Jackie Robinson file—follow Robinson's season with the Kansas City Monarchs, and keep the team apprised of his whereabouts. When Rickey asked him to arrange a meeting, Sukeforth told him that the timing was fortunate. Robinson had banged up his throwing arm and was out of the Monarchs' lineup for several games.

Sukeforth took the overnight train to Chicago, where the Monarchs were playing the American Giants, cabbed out to Comiskey Park, and leaned over the third base railing during batting practice to casually, inconspicuously invite Robinson to visit him in his hotel room. Rickey had stressed that the approach should be quiet and confidential. He did not want advance publicity to oblige him to sign Robinson, or induce other teams to sign him, either. That very afternoon, Robinson rode the freight elevator at the Stevens Hotel up to Sukeforth's room. Blacks were allowed in the hotel, but the sight of a black man coming to visit a white guest was so infrequent as to provoke remarks. Sukeforth wanted to keep Robinson's arrival quiet. That Robinson assented may be a sign that the idea was beginning to dawn on him, too. A man who had refused to move to the back of the bus would not usually consent to steal himself away in a freight elevator, except as a coconspirator.

Once admitted, their business was quickly and amicably accomplished. The Brooklyn Dodgers, said Clyde Sukeforth, were beginning a new team called the Brooklyn Brown Dodgers. Branch Rickey would like to speak to Jackie Robinson. Would Robinson be free to come to Brooklyn? Or would he prefer that Mr. Rickey come out to see him? Robinson chose to come to Brooklyn, and more or less immediately. He had a day or two off while his arm was healing. He told the Monarchs he would rejoin them in Kansas City in three days, took a morning train to New York, spent the night at a hotel in Harlem, and met Clyde Sukeforth in the lobby of 215 Montague Street on the morning of August 28, 1945, just two weeks after the surrender of Japan. A man as determined and intelligent—and as insightful—as Jackie Robinson must have suspected that Mr. Rickey had not invited him to Brooklyn solely to discuss the Brooklyn Brown Dodgers. The men ascended to the building's fourth floor. Clyde Sukeforth felt his shirt sticking to his chest as the floors clacked by, and said to himself, "Hot day."

Robinson was shown into Rickey's office, and Rickey rose to meet him. The general manager shifted his cigar into his left hand and stuck out his right to grasp Robinson's.

"Good to meet you, Mr. Robinson."

"Mr. Rickey."

The fish tank gurgled. Lincoln looked down somberly from his frame. The windows were open, and the late summer sounds of downtown Brooklyn put a din under their words—bus belches and taxi horns, the ringing of streetcars and the grinding of the elevated train. For fifteen, thirty seconds, almost a minute, the two men just looked across Branch Rickey's desk at each other, exchanging slow smiles.

"As if they were trying to get inside each other," recalled Clyde Sukeforth. "The air was electric in there. They just stared and stared at each other. Oh, what a pair, those two!"

There were the obvious differences in age, race, and region: between an old man and a young one, a white man and a black one, a Midwesterner who came to New York and a Southerner who came to California. As they shook hands, the two men might have automatically noted the difference between an old second-string catcher and one of the most versatile and accomplished athletes in American collegiate history.

But the quick comfort they found in each other's company suggests that it was more interesting for them to detect similarities.

Both men were dapper. They might have recognized in each other the determination of a boy from a modest family to dress with distinguishing taste and deliberate flourish. Rickey wore bow ties as broad as butterfly wings, and bright pocket squares that left an impression of jauntiness. Robinson wore trim sport coats and pastel open-necked knit shirts, Southern California style, which flattered his athletic form. He placed a squared white handkerchief in his breast pocket on almost all occasions.

Both men were religious. And both were Methodists, though Rickey was rather more regular in church attendance than Robinson (but then, Robinson often had to be at the ballpark by 11:00 A.M. on Sundays; Rickey had been released as a rookie by the Cincinnati Reds after he refused to play on Sundays). They were early risers and hard workers who did not end the day without praying.

Both men knew that they shared abhorrence for cursing, drinking, and adultery. They might commit an occasional slip on the first, just to make themselves understood in a roughhouse environment; they might make a rare exception, like locker room champagne, for the second; but they made no allowance for the third.

Both could be moralizers. They believed that hard work, discipline, obedience, and prayer were virtues, not just strategies. But both men could cherish and value the company of hard-drinking, coarse-talking adulterers (Leo Durocher or Roy Campanella) who also worked hard on the baseball field. Casey Stengel said of Rickey, "He never took a drink himself, but would sign a real drunkard if he could slide across home plate."

And both men could be sensitive to criticism. Hard workers often find it difficult to believe that their strenuous and untiring efforts could ever be wrong.

Rickey finally opened the conversation with a wag of his cigar.

"Do you have a girl, Jackie?"

"I'm not sure," said Robinson with a smile. He had proposed marriage to Rachel Isum; they spoke of a future together. But she was not so sure, and Robinson shared that uncertainty, that the roving life of a professional ballplayer did not make a man a good bet for a happy marriage.

"If you have the right girl in your life, Jackie, it makes all the difference." Rickey encouraged Robinson to get married.

"You will need the support," he said almost nonchalantly, "for all the trials that lie ahead." Rickey might have intended the sentence as the first signal flare for the plans he had in mind. But an American black man who could fairly expect to spend the rest of his life wrestling against racism might not read the same import into those words; he would have plenty of trials without major league baseball. Rickey then fixed his broad face and owlish gaze on the man across from him.

"Do you know why I wanted to meet you? Do you know why we brought you here?"

Robinson shrewdly chose not to assume anything beyond what he had been told, and told to keep to himself.

"I know that you are starting a team called the Brooklyn Brown Dodgers."

"No," said Rickey with a splay of his plump hand. "That's not why we brought you here. We want you to play, all right. We want you to play for the Brooklyn organization, Jackie. Perhaps in Montreal to start with."

Robinson knew there was no Negro League team in Montreal, and Rickey was not about to start one in a French-Canadian city (even a Negro league hockey team would have a better chance for success). Rickey could only be speaking of the Montreal Royals, the Dodgers' principal minor league team.

"Me, sir?" he said with a show of surprise. "Me, play for Montreal?"

"If you can make it," Rickey said with a show of his own. "And later on—also if you can make it—you'll have a chance to play with the Brooklyn Dodgers."

There, after so long a time, it was said in the open. The words rang out and fell almost visibly across Rickey's long desk. Robinson stayed silent. Rickey then rose to his feet, shifting his cigar to his left hand so he could thwack the palm of his right hand on his desk pad.

"I want to win the pennant, Jackie, and we need ballplayers to do it. Do you think you can do it?" A quick response would have seemed inauthentic bravado; and Robinson, with the superb restraint and timing of a great base runner, did not commit that error. He drew the string of the silence back among the three of them; he held the silence, almost in his hands, before speaking, finally saying only, "Yes."

Rickey was delighted. Rickey was refreshed. Rickey came out from behind his desk and paced before Robinson, who stayed seated in a high-backed leather conference chair. It will be rough, he said. There would be threats, taunts, and verbal abuse beyond any Robinson might have heard on a Southern California athletic field.

"I know you're a good ballplayer," said Rickey. Hitting, running, fielding—but this was something beyond. This was beanballs, high spikes, catcalls, and death threats. "I've got to know," he said, "if you've got the guts."

There was already a natural rhythm in the back and forth between the two men.

"Do you want a player," asked Robinson, "who doesn't have the guts to fight back?"

"I'm looking for a ballplayer," Rickey thundered at the opening, "with the guts *not* to fight back!" It was a masterful response; it called on that most combative of competitors to make restraint, not ferocity, the measure of his courage.

Rickey slipped off his jacket. White suspenders strained against the sides of his chest and stomach. He bent down to begin a sequence of impersonations: an unwelcoming white hotel clerk, an insulting white waiter, a surly white railroad conductor.

I'm sorry, Mr. Robinson. We have no rooms for your kind. You'll have to get you a room at the nigger hotel across town. Hey, boy, what do you think you're doing here? You know we don't serve your kind here. Get back there, boy. You know better. You know your kind can't sit in this car. Robinson looked up from his seat but did not flinch or, for that matter, rise. He stayed seated and contrived to look as unruffled as he had when harangued by a true turd of a racist bus driver in a small Texas town.

Rickey had the aspect of an actor; Rickey was, without doubt, one of life's great unscripted actors. He became a one-man repertory of racist ballplayers, sneering at

81

Robinson: *Hey, nigger boy. Scared of that ball, nigger boy? Hungry for some watermelon, nigger boy?* He crabbed his hands into claws that flashed fingers like spikes, turned up from a slide threatening to slice into Robinson's chin: *How do you like that, nigger boy?* For his finale, Rickey actually balled his right hand into a fist and aimed it at Robinson's head. The ballplayer's superb reflexes might have been slowed for a moment by sheer surprise. Rickey missed in any case—even as a catcher, he could not reliably hit a stationary target. Rickey sat down, winded. He understood, he said, that Robinson might be outraged off the field about taunts and threats. But he needed a man of "exceptional intelligence" who could "grasp and control his responsibilities."

"I need someone, Jackie," said Rickey, "who can carry that load. Above all," he said heavily, "you cannot fight back. That's the only way this experiment will succeed, and others will follow in your footsteps."

Robinson was, all at once, fascinated and moved by the slightly bulbous, ridiculous, and magnificent character who sat, deflated and tired, in a chair by his side. Years later, Robinson said that in that instant he had decided that he had to give Rickey his pledge for several flesh-and-blood reasons: for his mother, who had struggled across the country to raise her children in California's inexhaustible sunlight; for his brothers, Frank and Mack, who had missed, by merciless tricks of fate and time, the kind of chance that Branch Rickey had offered him on that day; for Rachel Isum, whom he intended to marry; for black youngsters across the country. And finally, he said, "I had already begun to feel I had to do it for Branch Rickey."

Rickey had a book he wanted to give Robinson. He picked up a vintage copy of Giovanni Papini's *Life of Christ* and opened it to a section he wanted to recommend to Robinson. Rickey read it out loud as the fish tank burbled and the bustle of Brooklyn clanged and jangled through the open windows four floors above Montague Street.

"'Ye have heard that it hath been said,'" Rickey began, "'An eye for an eye, and a tooth for a tooth. But I say unto you, that ye resist not evil. But whosoever shall smite thee on thy right cheek, turn to him the other also.'" Robinson would recall later that he kept his head down with instinctive respect during this scriptural reading, then lifted his head to meet Rickey's gaze.

"Mr. Rickey," said Jackie Robinson, his intense brown eyes burning and shining, "I have another cheek."

Branch Rickey was called the Mahatma for some of his worst qualities (his overbearing pomposity and insufferable certainty), not his best (his conviction, compassion, and capacity for friendship).* His feelings about India's nonviolent revolution and Mahatma Gandhi's philosophy of overturning raw force with the human spirit are unknown; he quoted Lincoln and La Guardia.

But like the genuine Mahatma, Rickey's choice for peaceful change was strategic as well as moral. The idea was not just to overwhelm one's adversaries, but to reach into their hearts and turn them around. A doubter, a dunce, even an outright bigot might dislike the idea of blacks in major league baseball. But he or she had to be drawn into the drama of a lone player daring beanballs and catcalls, darting around spikes on the base paths as he sought not only to win baseball games, but to defeat hatred and win over a nation. Games don't get any greater stakes than those.

Within a year, Rickey would sign Roy Campanella and Don Newcomb to minor league contracts and send them to the Dodgers' Class A team in Nashua, New Hampshire. The area was less cosmopolitan than Montreal, more explicitly small-town, *Our Town* minor league. Campanella and Newcomb could concentrate on base-

---

* Or, for that matter, his generosity, at least with Jackie Robinson. Rickey disliked spending money on marginal players. But in time he made Robinson the highest-paid member of the Brooklyn club—due reward, he said, for the increase in attendance he had stimulated—and kept his salary at that level even as Robinson began to age and his performance suffered.

ball, while the Dodgers could concentrate on them. They were the other most promising players Rickey's scouting had turned up. But Newcomb was young, and Campanella was unproven to Rickey's satisfaction. Rickey did not want another major league team to sign them. However, he did not want to bring them onto the same stage at the same time or place that he had set for Jackie Robinson. Rickey had anointed a knight to ride out first.

On October 23, 1945, before Fiorello La Guardia could make his liberal legend secure as he left office with a promise to force New York's major league teams to integrate their organizations, Branch Rickey Jr. and Hector Racine, the president of the Montreal Royals, introduced Jackie Robinson of Pasadena, California, to a press conference as the newest member of the Brooklyn Dodgers organization. He would open the 1946 season in Montreal; if he played well there, he would be brought to Brooklyn. It was left to Robinson to draw the point for Canadian reporters:

"Of course," he said, "I can't begin to tell you how happy I am that I am the first member of my race in organized baseball. I realize how much it means to me, my race, and to baseball. I can only say I'll do my very best to come through in every manner."

Rickey Jr. told the Canadian reporters that his father

was "not inviting trouble, but he won't avoid it if it comes.

"Some players with us may even quit. But they'll be back in baseball after they work a year or two in a cotton mill." (A threat that would be laughable today, it does suggest how many major league ballplayers in those days were believed to be Southern-born.)

The one man who had any authentic right to feel slighted by the signing instead gave Robinson and Rickey an ungrudging endorsement. Satchel Paige did not feel overlooked, but—again—pointedly excluded, this time for his age and independent character. The Dodgers had signed the young college man shortstop who played *behind* him, in all ways, to break baseball's color barrier. But Paige, more than any other man, had begun to bring that barrier down, pitch by pitch, year by year, with the brilliance of his play and the pull of his personality. He could have been forgiven a moment of pique and hurt. Instead, when white reporters sought him out on the barnstorming circuit in Los Angeles, Satchel Paige suppressed his disappointment and responded with unqualified class.

"They didn't make a mistake by signing Robinson," he told them. "They couldn't have picked a better man." Nor passed over a better one.

7

Minor Leaguer

T he three days that Jackie and Rachel Robinson
spent trying to cross the country four months
later conveys much about the United States in
the late winter of 1946.

They had cancelled the last few days of their honey-
moon to prepare for spring training in Daytona Beach,
Florida. At Mr. Rickey's request, Rachel would be the
only Dodger organization wife invited. Rickey did not
want the pining of newlyweds for each other to divert
Robinson's energies, and he sensed that Robinson's need
for the kind of support and companionship only Rachel
could provide would be profound.*

---

* The Dodgers had also signed a thirty-year-old Negro League pitcher
named John Wright who had enjoyed a couple of promising years before
the war. But Wright was rather clearly signed to room with Robinson. He
appeared briefly in just six games for the Royals that year, earned no

The team encouraged the newly married couple to fly. It was a gift, to spare them fatigue and, they hoped, the insult of segregated seating and bathrooms that were then the rule on trains and buses in the South. The Robinsons departed Los Angeles in a newspaper picture of optimistic elegance, Rachel in the ermine coat Jackie had bought her as a wedding present to stay warm in Montreal, Robinson himself in a new gray gabardine suit. They flew overnight, without incident, to New Orleans, landing at sunrise to connect with another flight in an hour's time that would take them to Pensacola, with connecting service on to Daytona. Rachel Robinson, who had spent all her life in Southern California, was shocked by the sight of the first signs she had seen of official segregation: "Whites Only" placards over the drinking fountains and toilets.

The Robinsons were bumped from the next flight to Pensacola—overbooked, said the airline, although they thought several seats were visibly available. Rachel and Jackie were both hungry, but the coffee shop in the New Orleans airport would not serve blacks. They said they could make sandwiches for the couple to eat. But they could not sit down at the counter; they would have to eat them out of their laps, perched in a "Colored Only" waiting area. Rachel Robinson gasped. She had

---

decisions, and had no earned run average. By the time organized baseball had integrated room assignments, most major stars had contracts providing for single rooms.

encountered racial hate in Southern California, but not the kind of almost humdrum, everyday discrimination that was encoded in official segregation. The Robinsons refused; they were still more angry than hungry.

The airline said that flights for Pensacola would resume in the evening, and suggested that the Robinsons wait at a hotel in the city. They were delivered to a squalid spot, creaky, grimy, and crawling with water bugs and cockroaches. Jackie Robinson knew the hotel, and hotels like it, from the Negro Leagues, but Rachel Robinson was frightened by the filth and would not let them sleep in the bed. They napped in their clothes, and covered themselves with newspapers.

The airline, of course, never called. The Robinsons had to go back to the airport on their own, and were finally added onto the last flight into Pensacola. When they landed, Jackie Robinson was paged. At first, he was relieved and delighted. He assumed that someone in the Dodgers must have worried over his whereabouts and called the airline, telling them that the Robinsons were very important passengers. But instead, the Robinsons were informed that a storm was coming and the plane had to be made lighter for more fuel. They would have to surrender their seats. As Jack and Rachel Robinson stood in stupefaction near the departure gate, a couple of people who had not been on the plane from New Orleans were put into their seats. The people—was it so surprising?—were white.

Now, there almost was a storm—Jackie Robinson. His wife was beyond tears. They were both beyond tired. They had been lied to, pushed around, and insulted. Their tickets were paid for; direct service was assured; yet they were already a day late because the airline had put white people on before them.

Robinson came close to a righteous eruption. But in the end, he realized that no remonstration would have gotten them seats on the airplane. Any demonstration might have gotten him arrested and tried, once again, for being "insubordinate, disrespectful, and discourteous." Robinson did not care about angering the airline. But he had made a promise to Branch Rickey; breaking that promise on the flight out to spring training, before so much as a pitch had been thrown, would be a breach of his faith. The Robinsons decided to complete their journey to Daytona Beach by bus—the speed and ease of airline travel were proving just too hard to take.

The first leg was sixteen hours to Jacksonville. The Robinsons struggled to sleep in reclining seats near the back of the bus, but at an unknown hour in the middle of the night, along a lonely stretch of Florida, the Robinsons were told that they had to move into the very last row of the bus, where the seats did not recline. White people wanted the seats they were in. Jackie Robinson's suit lapels were beginning to curl and curdle as he sat up stiffly and dozed in and out from stop to stop. Rachel

Robinson could not sleep—she could not close her eyes over her tears.

Sixteen hours to Jacksonville, and another sixteen to Daytona Beach. Branch Rickey told reporters straight-faced that Robinson had reported late because of "bad weather" along the route.

Robinson had a poor spring. Clay Hopper, the Montreal manager, knew that Branch Rickey was eager to see him win a starting spot, so Hopper moved Robinson around to each slot in the infield, from shortstop to first base to second base, then back to short. He wanted to see him displayed in all possible arrangements. But Robinson was so eager to impress that he pressed, and strained his throwing arm. His fielding stayed faultless, but his weakened arm made him, for the first time in his career, a defensive liability. It may also have thrown off the balance and timing of his batting stroke. Robinson was in a batting slump for most of the spring—except because no one had seen him hit, it didn't look like a slump: it looked as if Jackie Robinson couldn't hit.

Segregation laws prohibited the Robinsons from staying at the Riviera, the seaside hotel in which the white Royals were ensconced. Rickey sent his lieutenants into the black community of Daytona Beach and secured a room for the Robinsons in the home of one of the city's

most prominent physicians. The comfort and camaraderie of their accommodations did not quite make up
for the sting of the regulations that kept them separate
from the rest of the Royals.

Robinson's teammates stood apart and seemed a little
suspicious of his celebrity (most minor league rookies are
not trailed by reporters, or acclaimed by fans). Their own
chances to make the Montreal squad, or get promoted to
Brooklyn, were diminished when one Southern city after
another, Jacksonville; Savannah, Georgia; then Richmond,
Virginia, cancelled exhibition games because Robinson was
with the Royals, and local laws prohibited the integration
of players or crowds at public events. In one game, against
the St. Paul Saints in Sanford, Florida, Robinson hit a single, stole second base, and ran home on a single. A local
sheriff waited for him in the Royals' dugout, handcuffs
jangling, saying that Robinson would have to come out of
the game, or the game must be stopped. Under the city's
code, blacks and whites could not play on the same field.
Clay Hopper did not want to forfeit a game in which his
team had taken the lead, so he complied—telling Robinson that he had proven something with his hit, but had to
be removed for the good of the team.

DeLand, Florida, cancelled a game because they said
the lights were not working in the city's stadium. It was a
day game.

A few New York reporters sent back stories saying that
the plain fact was that Jackie Robinson had done little to

make the Montreal roster. If he had been a less publicized player, if he had not received a signing bonus, and if Branch Rickey had not tied up so much of his own prestige into his success, Robinson would have been sent down to Nashua, New Hampshire—or cut.*

But Rickey was unflagging. He sat in the front row of every Southern stadium in which the Dodgers played, cheering Robinson's fielding range and baserunning flair. It was during this vexing period that their mutual regard began to grow into emotional closeness. Rickey, more than any human being save for Rachel Robinson, knew about the range of pressures under which Robinson played. Even his stinted performance earned Rickey's admiration and renewed his determination to see Robinson win a chance to play for the Royals. Robinson had, Rickey made a point of telling the New York reporters, all

---

* Eventually, the competition for the best Negro League stars would become so intense that major league clubs would sign them directly. But the instinct at first was that even the best Negro League players needed seasoning in the minor leagues. This now appears patronizing. Why should the most complete performer of his time be stayed from entering the major leagues a season longer after he had already been held back by racism? But in 1946, Jackie Robinson himself believed that because Negro League teams played more exhibition baseball, even the best players needed experience in some of organized baseball's routines. Buck Leonard of the Kansas City Monarchs said that while the top stars of the Negro Leagues—men including Robinson, Satchel Paige, and Leonard himself—were the equal or more of any major leaguer, the general level of play in the Negro Leagues was closer to that of the high minors.

the physical and mental skills to play any position in the infield. "He'll hit," Rickey rather airily assured the regulars. "And he'll be quite a ballplayer. I'm sure of that."

Clay Hopper was from Mississippi. He lived there during the off-season; his family still owned a plantation there. Clay Hopper had not attended the press conference at which Jackie Robinson was unveiled as a member of the Montreal Royals; he was not invited, which was just as well, because he was not eager to be seen smiling with a black man in a photograph. Hopper had shaken Jackie Robinson's hand when he arrived in Florida, but only out of regard for Branch Rickey. Clay Hopper was the proud descendant of Confederates. He believed that God had marked all the peoples of the world with different colors because they were meant to be separate. He believed that black people could be kindly, lovable, musical, and noble, just not as smart, not as able, as whites. He did not blame blacks; he had grown up with blacks in Mississippi. Segregation was simply God's design, even if it was not Branch Rickey's.

One afternoon, Robinson was holding down third base in an exhibition and leapt to cover a line drive down the third base line, reaching his glove across his body to knock down the ball and pluck it up from the dirt in time to make a throw. Rickey, sitting behind the Royals dugout, was exultant.

"My gosh, Clay," he said, "did you see that? No other human being alive could have made that play." Clay

94

Hopper turned around to face his general manager with a look so severe it made him tremble to hold it. "Mr. Rickey, do you really think a nigger's a human being?"

So Clay Hopper was a racist. But Rickey also knew him to be a man of deeply inculcated courtesy. When Hopper first heard white people in Florida booing Robinson's appearance on a baseball field, he thought it was unnecessarily ill-mannered. The man was only trying to do the job he'd been hired to do. If Robinson could not play as well as white people, that would be proven soon enough—but people only debased themselves by booing. Robinson had not proved himself as a player, but he seemed to conduct himself as a gentleman. As the weeks of cancelled exhibitions proceeded, Hopper began to root for Robinson to turn some of those boos back around in the throats of such vulgar fans.

The Royals opened their season on April 18 against the Jersey City Giants. Roosevelt Stadium thumped with a brass band, circus clowns, and politicians, foot-stomping, whistles, cheers, and roars. When Jackie Robinson stepped out on the field, he would become the first black player of the twentieth century on the roster of a club affiliated with the major leagues. Thousands of black fans from Harlem, Brooklyn, Baltimore, and Philadelphia thronged in the grandstands; scores of reporters and photographers from Manhattan, Chicago, and Washington, D.C., lined up along the railings behind home plate.

Jackie Robinson came to bat in the first inning, played on by a chorus of encouraging cheers. He hit a slow ball that the Giants shortstop handled with quick and unexceptional skill. Robinson came up next in the third inning. Montreal runners were on first and second. The situation suggested a bunt, and Robinson was just the man to drop it; bunting was one of the few features of his batting game that had not suffered in spring training. But the Jersey City pitcher would not oblige. He winged a fastball toward Robinson, thrown as high as the *Montreal* splayed across his chest. When Robinson recognized the flight and speed of the ball, he tugged his bat back up with his forearms and struck the ball as it entered the strike zone. The ball rose rapidly, almost like a golf shot. An instant later, the sound of the hit seemed to trail—it had the crack of a tree being split in a lightning storm. The ball climbed into the sky, curled down as it approached Roosevelt Stadium's left field wall, and finally fell into a sea of upturned palms and grasping fingers, almost 340 feet away in the left field grandstands, for a three-run home run. The Jersey City crowd got to their feet to applaud history. And as Jackie Robinson trotted past third base, Clay Hopper patted him on the back— and whooped. "That's the way to hit the ball!" Just six weeks before, Hopper had to steel himself to be able to shake Robinson's hand.

In the fifth inning, Jackie Robinson did drop a bunt—dead-solid perfect, rolling to a stop along the first base line. He stole second base, then went to third on a ground out, staring down the shortstop to run by. Once he had claimed third base as his staging area, Robinson began to dance: he would take a few breakneck steps toward home, stop himself suddenly, as if on springs, then bolt back in time to beat a throw from pitcher Phil Otis. He did it once, twice, and began to dart down a third time when Phil Otis held up his delivery. "Balk!" cried the umpire, and this sent Robinson ambling home, a man who had turned a bunt into a run, base by base, with cunning, craft, and audacity. The Royals won the game 14 to 1. Jackie Robinson would get four hits, including a home run, steal two bases, and score four times. It was the best single pressure performance on an opening day that could be recalled by the reporters who had converged on Jersey City. Wendell Smith reported that when Rachel Robinson was finally able to thread her way through a phalanx of fans—Jackie Robinson fans, suddenly—outside the visitors' locker room, she patted his cheek softly. "Little man," she said, "you've had a busy day."

Jackie Robinson had perhaps the best single season of any player ever in the International League. He would be the league's Most Valuable Player in 1946, winning the batting title with a .349 average, driving in 66 runs, and scoring 113, more than any other player. The Royals would win the pennant by 18½ games, and the franchise would set a new attendance record: a million fans would come to their baseball park in De Lorimer Downs (a figure that must look unattainable to today's doomed Montreal Expos).

If luck was indeed the residue of design, then Robinson and the Dodgers were lucky that Branch Rickey had deigned to affiliate the club with the Royals. Montreal was simply the best big city in North America for Jackie Robinson to step into the game of organized baseball. Montreal fans marveled at the flair of his play—his very moves had some of the flash and slash of ice hockey—and were drawn by the drama of seeing Robinson defeat his adversaries and doubters.

Racism was scarcely unknown in Montreal. Quebec's antidraft riots during World War II had featured some vicious anti-Semitism. But Montreal cultivated a Parisian self-image. The city received Jackie Robinson as if he were a black American expat jazz musician in the Latin Quarter.* The city also had a large Jewish community in those years, with many ties to Brooklyn; they delighted in becoming a part of Robinson's story, too. Rachel Robinson said she could not recall a single incident of

---

* Sports in Montreal were already integrated, although not hockey. The Montreal Allouettes football team had a black running back—an American, Herb Trawick.

unpleasantness—much less race-baiting—during their months in Montreal: not where they lived, in the East End, not at any of the open-air concerts they attended on Mount Royal, and not at the ballpark. Branch Rickey had assigned Montreal a role in history, and the city cherished it.

The problems Robinson encountered were on the road, but not in the South (the Baltimore Orioles were the southernmost team in the International League until Havana entered in 1954). Syracuse was an especially rough stop. An unidentified player once put a black cat out onto the field to walk by the Montreal dugout, and this set off a chorus: "Hey, Jack, who's your cousin?" Robinson doubled, then scored on a single. As he turned by the Syracuse dugout, he permitted himself to call out, "I guess my cousin's pretty happy now!"

International League players were convinced that pitchers set a record for beanballs that year, most thrown at Robinson's chin. But this isn't reflected in a statistic. Robinson was vigilant to the threat, and usually managed to fall away from the pitch. Opposing players often came into second base with their spikes flashing toward his chest or chin. But newspapers in Montreal, Toronto, Buffalo, Newark, and other stops in the league were reluctant to report a pattern of assault if Robinson himself did not complain, and he did not.

Robinson enjoyed such a stellar season for Montreal in 1946 that if his play had not been regarded as a social experiment, he almost certainly would have been called up to the Dodgers in September. They were flailing just a couple of games behind the St. Louis Cardinals. A pinch hit, a couple of stolen bases—it's not hysterical to suggest that if the Dodgers had brought Jackie Robinson to Brooklyn late in the 1946 season, they could have won a pennant.

But Rickey was playing for a time beyond. The Royals opened the Little World Series against the Louisville Colonels—the team he might have played for if the Boston Sox had had the nerve to sign him. The conduct of some of the Colonels ratified the luck that had been the residue of Robinson being signed by Branch Rickey.

Several Louisville players said they would not take the field with a black man. Several city officials said they did not know that blacks and whites on the same field of play didn't risk public safety, and they might have to act. But over the six months of the season, Jackie Robinson had become the most heralded player in the International League, a national enthusiasm. The Colonels did not want to incite an incident that would make Louisville look irredeemably minor league—and drive away the largest crowds, white and black, they were ever likely to draw. The parent club in Boston told the Colonels that they would play the Royals, including Jackie Robinson, or they could shop around for another major league affil-

iation. The Red Sox might not have the decency or daring to sign black players on their own. But they had the
good sense (or, at least, public relations sense) not to
openly oppose a black man who was brave enough to
take the field alone against a team of white men.

The taunts and abuse reached a new low in Louisville.
Robinson, who at that point was almost accustomed to
hearing encouraging cheers from grandstands in
Rochester, Jersey City, Toronto, and Baltimore, was
sluggish at the start. The Royals won the first game, then
lost the next two.

But by the time they returned to Montreal, Robinson
was hitting .400 and the Royals were unstoppable. When
they won the last game of the Little World Series, fans
tumbled and danced out onto the field of De Lorimer
Downs and ran for Jackie Robinson—who, at that point,
was not threatened by such throngs. Sam Maltin, a
Canadian socialist political writer who became a good
friend of the Robinsons and filed occasional stories on
Jackie's season for the Negro press in the United States,
wrote the most-quoted line of that day, one of the most
quoted in sports chronicles: "It was probably the only
day in history that a black man ran from a white mob
with love instead of lynching on its mind."

Clay Hopper took both of Robinson's hands in his
own and, perhaps for the first time in his life, looked lev-
elly and directly into the eyes of a black man. "It's been
an honor to be your manager, Jackie," said Clay Hopper.

"You are a complete ballplayer, and a real gentleman." Montrealers swarmed around them. They lifted Jackie Robinson up from the field and took him onto their shoulders, raising him up and down as they took up a singsong chant: *"Il a gagné ses epaulettes"* (He has earned his stripes).

So much of Branch Rickey's plan had worked according to his design. He had found in Jackie Robinson a player who even exceeded his hopes, a complete and brilliant ballplayer who not only performed with skill and nerve, but also carried the aura of a winner. Luck may be the residue of design. But athletes can believe that luck is the residue of destiny. They believed, as fervently as soldiers, that luck is a substance that just stuck to certain people. From high school to college to the Kansas City Monarchs and then the Montreal Royals, Jackie Robinson had never been anything less than a champion. Luck seemed to attach itself around his shoulders.

But here is where Rickey's high-mindedness may have misinformed his judgment. He had planned that once the Dodgers had seen Jackie Robinson's winning ways close up, they would clamor to bring him onto their roster. But no baseball player roots for someone younger to compete for his job.

By the time spring training opened in 1947, all of the ten top hitters of the International League the season before had been promoted to the major leagues. But not the league's most valuable player, Jackie Robinson. In fact, the the major league owners had voted 15 to 1 (Branch Rickey alone opposed) to continue the ban on admitting blacks to the major leagues.

Rickey urged Robinson not to take the vote as a personal insult. How could he not? The owners could have had no one but Jackie Robinson in mind as they renewed the prohibition. Sixteen months after Robinson and John Wright had signed major league contracts, the Dodgers had signed three more black players to their minor league system.* No other major league organization had signed even one.

Rickey had arranged for the Dodgers and their principal farm clubs to spend most of spring training in Cuba and Panama. He wanted to avoid the irritations and cancellations that had been caused by segregation laws in the American South. However, Rickey still insisted that his black players stay in the dorms of a Cuban military school, rather than with the rest of the team in Havana's opulent seaside Hotel Nacional. Rickey wanted to avoid inflaming any unpleasantness with Southern American tourists. The decision tested Robinson's regard for Branch Rickey just a bit.

Rickey also told Clay Hopper to give Robinson a first

---

* Roy Campanella, Don Newcomb, and thirty-six-year-old Negro League pitcher Roy Partlow.

baseman's glove. Pee Wee Reese was set at shortstop; Eddie Stanky was becoming a fixture at second. Rickey did not want to bring Robinson onto the roster as a pinch hitter or runner. It would lack impact, and probably disgruntle Robinson. The best chance Jackie Robinson stood to crack the 1947 Dodger lineup would be at first base. Robinson told reporters that he understood that the decision to promote him to the Dodgers (or not) was personal. With more benevolence of spirit than was necessary—or perhaps even sincere—he told New York reporters, "If the Dodgers don't want me, there would be no point in forcing myself on them. I wouldn't want to feel that I was doing anything that would keep them from winning."

While Robinson was displaying a major league ability to turn reporters away with bromides, several Brooklyn players were plotting to force their prejudices on Rickey and the Dodgers. At one point, a petition was prepared; no copy exists today. It contained the names of several players—the list expanded and contracted over days and weeks—who said they did not wish to play on the same team as Jackie Robinson or, it was implied, any other black player. Pitchers Hugh Casey and Kirby Higbe were part of the group. So were Bobby Bragan, a backup catcher, and outfielders Dixie Walker and Carl Furillo (from Pennsylvania—the only Northerner among them).

At first, Pee Wee Reese was part of the group, too. Then, as the spring proceeded, he thought the matter

through—or perhaps just *thought,* rather than only react-
ing with ingrained intolerance. Reese had already sacri-
ficed three years of his playing career to help fight a war.
He did not want to sacrifice even a month more to fighting what he sensed, in the end, was the path of history.
Besides, he had seen for himself that Robinson was an
exceptional fielder and base runner, and, Robinson was
now being prepared to play first base, not shortstop.
Reese's estimation of Robinson was no longer compli-
cated by rivalry. The two men would eventually become
close friends. Learning that Pee Wee Reese was once
briefly associated with those who opposed Robinson
does not diminish Reese's rapid discovery of fortitude.
On the contrary, it reminds us that good people have the
character to change the convictions of a lifetime.

Rickey and his manager, Leo Durocher, got word of the
petition and were appalled. More, they were *angry.*
Rickey was prepared to wrestle with opposing general
managers and the commissioner of baseball. He actually
looked forward to shouting down the protests and
doubts of Southern Democrats, Yankee bigots, Ku
Kluxers, and other assorted cowards, haters, and clucks.
But not his own Dodgers.

Rickey deployed Leo Durocher to this front. The
Dodger manager was not known for his moral force.
He was an accomplished, committed, and charming

scoundrel, egotistical and irascible, a gambler, scalawag, and a gam-chaser.

And yet, all of that lent Durocher a kind of character. He could be a bully. But he had no record as a bigot. Eleanor Roosevelt, Pete Seeger, or The Weavers might have reminded the players that it was their moral responsibility to accept a man of a different color in their midst. Leo rousted his players out of slumber (or revelry) one night during an exhibition stand in Panama City and marched them into the kitchen of the team's hotel (Robinson and the other black players being elsewhere encamped). Leo lit his long filtered cigarettes with a gold Dunhill (subtly reminding the players that he had tasted of the riches of the World Series and Hollywood starlets; most of them had not), and flicked flecks of ash off the expansive gold silk of his Sulka gown. Rocking back on a kitchen stool, Durocher was positively leonine.

"Listen," Leo told his Dodgers, "I don't care if this guy is white, black, green, or has stripes like a *fucking zebra*. If I say he plays, *he plays*. He can put an awful lot of *fucking money* in our pockets. Take your petition and *shove it up your ass*. This guy can take us to the World Series, and so far we haven't won *dick*."

Shortly after Durocher's delicately phrased appeal to reason, Branch Rickey called Hugh Casey, Kirby Higbe, Dixie Walker, Bobby Bragan, and Carl Furillo into his own top-floor suite for a private consultation. Rickey's purpose was to remind the players, un-Mahatma-like, that there was a potential price for their opposition. "The time for education and persuasion is over," he announced. If the players did not want to stay on the same team as a black man, they would be traded. But, Rickey advised them, if the players believed that there was a team in major league baseball that would not soon sign its own black players once they had seen the likes of Jackie Robinson, then Campanella and Newcomb, they were naïve. A really smart player, he assured them, would adjust his way of thinking.

Bobby Bragan told Rickey he was sorry to dispute him—it was just the way he felt because he had grown up in Birmingham. Rickey assured Bragan that he could be traded—and feel free to *really* grow up elsewhere. Rickey was especially pointed and stern with Carl Furillo, the one Northerner of the group, who was from central Pennsylvania. *Your parents came here from Sicily, right, Carl?* Rickey inquired. *Do you think everyone in America is happy that they ever let Sicilians in?* It was an especially savage question in the days of Lucky Luciano.

Kirby Higbe would be traded. Dixie Walker would write Rickey a polite-sounding letter asking to be traded; he did not so much as mention race or Jackie Robinson ("for reasons I prefer not to go into . . ." he wrote). Rickey refused to trade Walker—which reminded all the other Dodgers that Rickey could send them away or make anyone stay.* The rebellion died. The Dodgers had returned to New York on April 10 and were in the sixth inning of their last exhibition game against the Royals when Jackie Robinson bunted into a double play while one of Branch Rickey's press flacks strolled through the Ebbets Field press box, slowly doling out copies of a short statement signed by Branch Rickey. The expanse of surrounding white on the paper afforded the two lines a dramatic spotlight:

"The Brooklyn Dodgers," it said, "today purchased the contract of Jackie Roosevelt Robinson from the Montreal Royals. He will report immediately."

After the game, Clay Hopper took Robinson into the home locker room, where the Brooklyn clubhouse manager showed him a hook on which he could hang his clothes—no lockers would be available until after Mr. Rickey made the final roster cuts—and handed Robinson a uniform that he thought would fit just about right, with 42 in blue felt numbers on the back. Today that number is retired on every club in major league baseball, in homage to the man who had to hang his first uniform on a hook.

---

* Hell—Walker had hit .319 the previous season.

8

The Season

What newspaper readers saw was the picture of a wide-eyed, wide-shouldered, dark-skinned twenty-eight-year-old, his hat with the looping signature *B* over the brim set back slightly from over his forehead, sitting on the Brooklyn bench and crowned with the hands of laughing and excited youngsters. A black man in a white home jersey, wearing the Brooklyn *B*, along with Reese, Reiser, and Dixie Walker. He signed his name with quick and practiced aplomb on Ebbets Field scorecards and scraps of paper, in the margins of newspapers, and on the green undersides of brims of small *B* hats:

Good luck
Jackie R. Robinson

A reporter told Wendell Smith he was impressed by Robinson's poise with fans, and Smith reminded him that Jackie Robinson had been signing autographs since he was sixteen years old. Robinson was taken over to shake hands with various Brooklyn politicians and the borough president; several were wearing buttons that read "I'm for Robinson." Robinson told the politicians and reporters, "I just wanted to be treated like any other player." In the Brooklyn locker room, the Dodgers' interim manager, Clyde Sukeforth,* went over the Boston Braves batting order with his players, and offered suggestions on trying to get a hit off Boston's great right-hand starter, Johnny Sain. The second portion was particularly sketchy: no one could hit Johnny Sain in those years. As the men milled back to their lockers, Sukeforth asked Robinson, "How are you feeling?"

"Fine," said Jackie Robinson. He had struggled with a sore right arm through the spring.

"Good," said the man who had brought him into Branch Rickey's office eighteen months before. "You're starting at first base." He said it only to Robinson, but word spread in the close confines of the locker room. A few players—he didn't know everyone's name yet, so

---

* Leo Durocher had been suspended from baseball for a year for exchanging insults with the Yankees' general manager, Lee McPhail, over which man had closer ties to professional gamblers. It is hard to know who was the pot, and who was the kettle.

when he told the story later that day to Wendell Smith, he could only remember Gene Hermanski and Ralph Branca—came over to wish him good luck. Not congratulations, but good luck. Robinson knew that trials were ahead. The first was to hit Johnny Sain's fastball.

That morning of Tuesday, April 15, 1947, New York's newspapers reported that Rudolf Hess had been returned to Auschwitz to be hanged for arranging the murder of 4,000,000 people and stripping their corpses of gold teeth and hair. Frank Sinatra had slugged a man who called him a dago sonofabitch. A poll of sportswriters revealed that most had picked the St. Louis Cardinals and Boston Red Sox to repeat as pennant winners. The government of Syria said it did not know what had happened to the 17,000 Jews who had been listed in the country's last census. The exotic dancer Satira (born in Indiana with the name Patricia Schmidt) told reporters from her prison cell in Havana that she had shot her boyfriend, Chicago mob lawyer John Lester Mee, because he had promised to marry her but neglected to mention that he was already married. "I'm so sorry I shot him," she said. "We were terribly in love."

Johnny Sain was virtually unhittable. But not unbeatable. Jackie Robinson, batting second behind second baseman

Eddie Stanky, swung too soon trying to hit a Sain fastball in the first inning and flied out to center field. In the fourth inning, he took a bare slice out of another fastball and dribbled it without menace to Sibby Sisti,* the Boston shortstop, who threw him out. Robinson handled the throws he received at first base competently, but without flourish. Eddie Stanky could see that the position was so new to him that Robinson still had to tap the heel of his right foot back against the bag as he prepared to take the throw. Robinson noticed that each time he trotted in from the infield when Brooklyn prepared to come to bat, Dodgers catcher Bruce Edwards clapped him on the back or right forearm.

Eddie Stanky led off the Dodgers seventh inning by drawing a walk. Robinson came to bat for the third time, and a sacrifice bunt to move Stanky into scoring position was clearly in order. Robinson improved on his orders.

Sain hurled the pitch hard and high over the center of the plate, trying to force Robinson to pop the ball up— where the catcher might snare it and keep Eddie Stanky at first base—rather than down into the ground, setting Stanky in motion toward second. Robinson ran the fingers of his right hand up to the thick end of his bat, barely skimming the column, and pulled his left hand

---

* Not a great player. But one of the great names in baseball history.

back on the knob of the bat, so when it met Johnny Sain's fastball, the bat snapped back into Robinson's palm. The bunt took the sting out of Sain's fastball. The pitch hit flat, like a bird flying into a brick wall, and Robinson steered the ball along the first base line almost as if he had put a string on it.

Sain broke from the pitcher's mound to cover first base. Boston first baseman Earl Torgeson ran in to pick up Robinson's bunt. Robinson sprinted from his standing start along that same baseline, deliberately running along the *inside* of the white line. When Torgeson wheeled around to throw the ball back to Sain at first base, he could not see where Sain stood. Robinson's round shoulders blocked his view. Torgeson threw the ball where he thought it ought to go. But as he let it go, he saw that Robinson was running with his arms splayed away from his body, elbows up like a high jumper striding into a takeoff. The ball grazed off Robinson's right elbow. It bounced off into right field foul territory, like a small coin rolling away down a subway platform. Stanky saw this as he turned around second and broke for third base. Robinson looked over his right shoulder as he neared first, saw the ball sitting up on the right field grass, as solitary as a white orchid on a prom dress, and began to dash for second. Both Dodgers pulled in safe. Pete Reiser then came up, laced a beautiful curving line drive that smacked off the left field wall, and brought Stanky and Robinson around to score. Brooklyn won Opening Day, 5 to 3.

• • •

Accounts of the game would properly praise Pete Reiser for his timely hit. But Dodgers coaches and players were taken by the ways in which Robinson had turned a sacrifice bunt into a play that put two runners into position to score with a single stroke. A home run would have left an impression of Robinson's power. But the precision of his bunt and the ingenuity of his baserunning gave a glimpse of the quality of Robinson's baseball mind. Some of the most bigoted white stars had had to concede the obvious over the years—that there were many talented black ballplayers. But this rational observation was often encased in another bigoted belief—that black ballplayers lacked the aptitude to truly understand the fine points that made baseball distinctive. No black ballplayer in America needed to disprove this delusion. Jackie Robinson did, nevertheless.

In the clubhouse, Robinson told reporters that he was mostly disheartened about not getting a hit off Johnny Sain.

"Is Sain the best pitcher you ever faced?" the flock of reporters asked. Robinson paused and smiled shyly.

"Well—er-r-r," he finally said. "I've hit against Feller, you know." Bob Feller, the young phenom of the Cleveland Indians.

Robinson's smile recognized what had gone without remark until then: many top black ballplayers had already faced their white counterparts in exhibition games. White players could not insist it was somehow wrong to play alongside blacks as long as they were willing to play against them in cash-producing exhibitions.

Robinson kept returning to how impressed he had been by Johnny Sain's pitching. "If they're all like this," he said, "I'm going to have a tough time making this league." Pee Wee Reese overheard Robinson's remarks and came by his locker. It was the first real exchange between two men whose images will soon be bronzed together in Brooklyn.

"Don't judge 'em all by Sain," Pee Wee told him. "You were looking at one of the best."

Wendell Smith had been hired by Branch Rickey to be Robinson's traveling companion while he covered the story of his first season in the major leagues for a string of black-owned newspapers. Smith drove Jackie and Rachel Robinson (and their infant son, Jack Jr.) back to their hotel in Manhattan's Herald Square, and remembered Robinson turning around as they crossed over the Brooklyn Bridge to speak to his wife, sitting with their new son in the backseat.

"The fellas were actually pretty swell," he told her. "I guess now it's all up to me." He turned to Smith and mused: "Five years of this will be fine. I hope to make a way for little Jackie. We'd like to try to begin building a home on the outskirts of Los Angeles next year.

"I know that I have a certain responsibility to my race,

but I've got to try not to feel that way about it because it would be too much of a strain. . . . I also know that I've got to hit. I'm going to hit, all right, and I'm not going to worry at any time."

Judy Holliday starred in *Born Yesterday* on Broadway, Ingrid Bergman was playing *Joan of Lorraine,* and the Trapp Family Singers, who had fled Nazi-occupied Austria, opened a four-week stand at their music camp in Stowe, Vermont. "Edelweiss" was not a part of their act. The song would not be written until Rodgers and Hammerstein composed it for the musical they would make about the family twelve years later. Marshall Field's liberal daily *PM* told its readers that "For 400,000 residents of Harlem, the benefits of democracy are not easy to find. They are some 17 per cent of the whole population of the city who, with rare exception, are Jim Crowed by unwritten law into poverty and isolation."

Columnist Billy Rose shared what he said was his anecdotal, empirical poll of the ten men whom women found to be the most attractive in America. Gregory Peck was the virtually unanimous winner (and might be still). Kirk Douglas and Hank Greenberg were the only Jews (and Greenberg the only one with a Jewish name). Cesar Romero was the only Latin. No black man was so much as mentioned. Rose's own choice was Secretary of State Ed Stettinius, an illustrious-looking, superficial, silver-haired nonentity.

Ed Stettinius?

• • •

The Dodgers drew 37,000 people for a Friday night, April 18, game at the Polo Grounds against the Giants. Jackie Robinson hit his first major league home run. The next day, more than 52,000 people swarmed into the Polo Grounds, the largest attendance figure in the ballpark's history. By April 24, Jackie Robinson was hitting .429 on the season. The *Baltimore Afro-American, Pittsburgh Courier, Chicago Defender,* and other black newspapers detailed each of Robinson's at bats as a separate feature, as if each time Robinson came to the plate, he took another step across the moon—which, in a way, he had. The *Afro-American* reported that most of the major white-owned newspapers in Florida had deleted all mention of Robinson's hits, runs, and stolen bases from their game stories. It was as fruitless as looking for news about Soviet famines and purges in *Pravda*.

On April 22, the Dodgers opened a three-game series at home against the Philadelphia Phillies. The Phillies turned out to be the kind of racist trolls that Branch Rickey had impersonated for Robinson in his office a year and a half before.

The Phillies were managed by an Alabamian named Ben Chapman who had played for the Yankees in the early 1930s. Chapman hit a respectable .302 over those years. But he was better remembered in Yankee Stadium for spitting anti-Semitic slurs at the fans, which, especially in New York, is the sign of a dedicated bigot, a remarkable ignoramus, or some incomparable combination of both. Reading through Ben Chapman's history today, you are inclined to wonder: Why would a major league club ever hire a half-bright bigot to manage their team?

Nine players took the field for Brooklyn. Chapman instructed his players to turn a torrent of ethnic abuse on Robinson. "To see if he can take it," Chapman said.

Our present-day imaginations may now be happily underdeveloped in conceiving racial epithets such as those spewed from the Philadelphia bench when Robinson approached the plate. In his 1972 autobiography, *I Never Had It Made*, Robinson's recollection was vivid and specific. Each epithet still pierces:

> *"Hey, nigger, why don't you go back to the cotton field where you belong?"*
>
> *"They're waiting for you in the jungles, black boy!"*
>
> *"Hey, snowflake, which one of those white boys' wives are you dating tonight?"* (Perhaps—probably—they did not say *dating*.)
>
> *"We don't want you here, nigger!"*
>
> *"Go back to the bushes!"*

Each racial insult was shouted loudly, without apology, self-consciousness, or conscience. Other Dodgers (even some Phillies) would remember hearing hideous references to thick lips, thick skulls, and syphilis sores. Robinson strode to the plate each time without averting his gaze or awarding a glance to the Philadelphia bench. When he took up his position at first base, just fifty feet from the visitors' dugout, the Phillies would wait until Robinson had turned toward the infield to take his warmup throws before striking up the chorus of name-calling and race-baiting. It was, perhaps, the only small sign of shame that day from the Phillies: they would call a man a nigger, but they could not bring themselves to say it to his face. Robinson would keep his face toward the field while the curses cascaded around his ears, both cheeks turned away. In the eighth inning, Jackie Robinson hit a single, stole second, and got to third base on an overthrow, from where a hit by Gene Hermanski sent him home. He scored the only run of the day, defeating Ben Chapman's Phillies 1 to 0.

But Robinson's sense of triumph was small. The hurt had simply been too great to be soothed away by a single; or, for that matter, a home run.

"For one wild and rage-crazed minute," Robinson wrote in 1972, "I thought, 'To hell with Mr. Rickey's "noble experiment"' . . . I was, after all, a human being. What was I doing here turning the other cheek as though I weren't a man?" Robinson said he wanted to "stride over to that Phillies dugout, grab one of those white sons of bitches and smash his teeth with my despised black fist."

Robinson's shoulder was sore the next day. But he kept that pain to himself, too, because he wanted to play—wanted to show the Phillies, show his own Dodgers, show *himself* that he would not be driven off by slurs, insults, or spikes.

Rickey had been wrong in figuring that Robinson's outstanding play in Montreal would start a drumbeat aboard the Dodgers to bring him onto the Brooklyn roster. But he still believed that the Dodgers would begin to feel themselves bound up in Jack's daily array of trials.

In the first inning, Eddie Stanky grounded out to second base. As soon as he passed Jackie Robinson, who was on his way to the batter's box, the screeches and taunts began to rise from the Philadelphia bench. *Hey, nigger! That ball ain't no watermelon, boy! You can't play with white boys, you know that! Back to the jungle, nigger boy!* Robinson continued his purposeful walk into position without any outward sign that he had heard this hateful chorale. His step was steady; his eyes were almost implausibly focused on home plate. But Stanky— *Alabamian Eddie Stanky*—had reached his breaking point. He popped back up from the Dodger bench like a challenged bantam rooster and called across the field to his fellow Alabamian, Ben Chapman: "Hey, you yellow-bellied coward! Why don't you pick on somebody who can fight back?"

* * *

The torrent of epithets that Chapman's Phillies let loose on Jackie Robinson had been so obvious and obnoxious that the commissioner of baseball, Hap Chandler, stepped in with an edict: he would fine, suspend, or banish any player who couldn't express himself with a perfectly vivid profanity that did not invoke a man's race.

Ben Chapman said he would comply. But he defended his razzing of Robinson as being part of the game, like sliding into a man's legs to break up a double play. The idea was to unnerve and distract. You called a man who was sensitive about his weight "the Hindenburg," a man who played with an injury "gimp," and a man who had a sharp profile "Jew-nose." If nothing so obvious was available, you shouted, "Hey, your wife was great in the sack last night." It meant nothing, said Chapman. Baseball's major stars might be treasured civic figures in their communities. But on a baseball field, Joe DiMaggio was disparaged as a "wop," Stan Musial was assailed as a "polack," and Hank Greenberg was called a "kike" (although at that point in each man's career, perhaps only by Ben Chapman).

But Chapman's attempt to make his taunts seem like just another gesture of equality accorded Robinson sounded puny and ridiculous in the din that had been heard from the Philadelphia dugout. Branch Rickey told reporters that Chapman had actually rendered the Dodgers a great service. "He solidified and unified thirty men, not one of whom was willing to sit by and see someone kick around a man who had his hands tied behind his back."

At the same time, the sight of a black man wearing floppy wool Dodgers flannels had begun to stir up an assortment of lunatics and haters across the country who were apparently eager to expend what small powers of literacy they possessed in sending threats and slurs to Jackie Robinson.

Ugly mail started to pour into Ebbets Field. Few copies survive today. What the team didn't dispatch into the trash, it turned over to the police. Robinson himself had no sentimental reason to hold onto such screeds. He saved the prayers people sent to him, the note from the elderly white woman in South Carolina who said, "I'm rooting for you," the letters of cheer and encouragement from Brooklynites and Southerners, rabbis and ministers. He saved crayoned greeting cards sent in from school classes and Hebrew schools—Jackie Robinson saved virtually anything sent by a child. But he could not imagine that the racist rants of bigots and cranks should be saved as artifacts of history; he was trying to change history. Two specific threats that arrived at Ebbets Field made it into news accounts: "Next time you take the field, nigger, I'll kill you." And: "Get out of baseball or else." There were also threats to kidnap and harm Rachel Robinson and Jackie Jr.

If there was ever a time at which Jackie Robinson doubted that he had the nerve to proceed with Branch Rickey's plan—or that the goal of integrating the major leagues was worth the agony and anguish—it was probably during the first two weeks of May 1947. The Dodgers began an extended road trip. The first stop was Philadelphia.

Herb Pennock, Philadelphia's general manager, had the enlightened and tactful attitude of his field manager. He phoned Branch Rickey just before the series opened and said, "You just can't bring that nigger here with the rest of your team, Branch. We're just not ready for that sort of thing." Pennock suggested that the Phillies would not take the field if Robinson were in the Brooklyn lineup. Rickey told Pennock that it would please him greatly if the Phillies forfeited the series. It would save the Dodgers the expense and uncertainty of actually trying to win any ball games.

The Phillies backed down, but not the town. When the Dodgers arrived on May 9, the Benjamin Franklin Hotel, their usual Philadelphia residence, refused to accept Jackie Robinson as a guest. Harold Parrott, the Dodgers' traveling secretary, was outraged. But his players were sleepy. Swallowing his hurt and pride, Robinson agreed to be housed at a black-owned hotel several blocks away.*

When the Dodgers arrived at Shibe Park, a new form of aggravation was waiting: *Ben Chapman wanted to have his picture taken with Jackie Robinson.* Chapman had not apologized for his malicious abuse of Robinson. But Robinson's strength and dignity had shown up Chapman as a bully and a fool, the dopey and cruel manager of a second-rate ball club. Chapman worried that he had made himself just about as popular as Ezra Pound. He needed a favor, and Branch Rickey was willing to grant it if it bought the Phillies' support for the continued integration of blacks into major league baseball. It would be hard for Philadelphia to threaten a boycott after they had to beg Jackie Robinson to save their manager's skin with a staged smile.

So Robinson complied—as a favor to Rickey. Ben Chapman seemed nervous. The Philadelphia photographer called for a handshake. But Harold Parrott wanted to save his star from swallowing at least one more small turd of humiliation. He held a baseball bat between the two men, which they mutually grasped. The pose was

---

* Thereafter the Dodgers stayed at the more luxurious Warwick Hotel, which did accept black guests. Robinson was acclaimed by his teammates. If this was the noble experiment Branch Rickey had in mind, they were all for it.

not previously known in the visual vocabulary of sports photographs. Robinson said nothing to reporters. Twenty-five years later he wrote, "I can think of no occasion where I had more difficulty in swallowing my pride and doing what seemed best for baseball and the cause of the Negro in baseball . . ."

(Dixie Walker, another Alabamian, murmured to Harold Parrott, "I never thought I'd see Ben swallow shit like that." Chapman, by the way, would be fired by the Phillies in the middle of the following year. He would never manage again.)

Robinson might have regretted his good show of graciousness during the game that followed. The Philadelphia newspapers had run stories about some of the mail and phone calls threatening Jackie Robinson's life. When he came to bat, several Phillies in the dugout—away from the field of play, where they might have been sighted and admonished by an umpire—leveled their bats at Jackie Robinson, squinted down phantom gun sights, and went *rat-a-tat-tat*, like machine guns.

But back in New York, the *Herald-Tribune* ran a story by their legendary sports editor, Stanley Woodward, who reported that unnamed National League players had hatched a plan to boycott Jackie Robinson. The cabal was reportedly centered among the St. Louis Cardinals.

Woodward took the artistic liberty of recreating a

speech that National League Commissioner Ford Frick was said to have delivered to the Cardinal players:

"I do not care if half the league strikes. Those who do it will encounter quick retribution. They will be suspended, and I don't care if it wrecks the National League for five years. This is the United States of America, and one citizen has as much right to play as another."

Frick confirmed the sentiment. But he was quick to correct the impression that he had ever uttered those words (unsuspected eloquence indeed from the man who, as commissioner of baseball, would put an asterisk by Roger Maris's 61 home runs), or had ever even talked to the Cardinals.

All these years later, it is not clear that there was anything more to Stanley Woodward's story than a little overheard loose talk. The best known members of the 1947 Cardinals have denied the story. Stan Musial, who would become a friend of Jackie Robinson, has always maintained that if there was any plan to refuse to play the Dodgers, the plotters kept it from him. St. Louis could not have mounted much a boycott without their stellar player.

Dick Sisler, a fledgling player on the 1947 Cardinals, told Jules Tygiel for his fine 1997 book, *Baseball's Great Experiment: Jackie Robinson and His Legacy*, "Very definitely there was something going on at the time whereby they said they weren't going to play." Sisler said older players alone were involved.

Tygiel points to the Cardinals as "a logical fulcrum"

for any strike. Many of their players were from the South. The rivalry between Brooklyn and St. Louis had become fierce (they had tied for first place in 1946, with the Cardinals winning the playoff series 2 games to 1), and aggravated by familiarity. Branch Rickey had built the St. Louis team before being brought to Brooklyn. Both clubs bore the stamp of his baseball convictions—speed, pitching, and character.

But the Cardinals were also the team that could be most easily caricatured by flashy New York newspaper columnists looking to display their city's superior high-mindedness. St. Louis was then the southernmost major league team. The area was segregated, conservative, religious. Brooklyn considered itself polyglot (although certainly segregated block by block) and progressive. Stanley Woodward's own words in reporting that the St. Louis plot had been averted betray an Eastern urban smugness at which New Yorkers may be singularly accomplished:

"It can now be honestly doubted," Woodward wrote, "that the boys from the Hookworm Belt will have the nerve to foist their quaint sectional folklore on the rest of the country." "The *rest of the country*" included Boston, Syracuse, Philadelphia, and other northern cities that could make St. Louis look as refined as classical Athens.*

---

* And the St. Louis Cardinals would have black players well before New York's own Yankees signed their first, Elston Howard, in 1955. Eight years later he would become the AL's first black MVP.

• • •

This was Jackie Robinson's hardest, darkest time. The Dodgers had arranged for him to live in the McAlpin Hotel on Herald Square. The Robinsons loved the surroundings of glitter and excitement flashing outside their window. But they were living in one small room, filled by a squalling infant son. There was no stove on which to heat the baby's milk, and no private place in which to change his diapers. Club functionaries, favor seekers, and reporters came calling early in the morning and on off days during which he craved sleep. Robinson was a Californian, accustomed to seeing the sun descend over a blue ocean, not a thin ribbon of quicksilver blocked by concrete columns, congested streets, and thickets of blank-faced people. His mail held death threats. The playing field, which had been a source of solace all his life, now bristled with beanballs, catcalls, boycotts, and—almost worst of all—strikeouts. Jackie Robinson was in a batting slump.

At the moment he was living and performing under the greatest scrutiny, his great skills had never been so strained. His right shoulder throbbed. His batting eye could not yet lock on the rotation of a major league curveball. When he toed in at the batter's box, a chorus of taunts and tirades scorched his ears. While other players scoured the grandstands for blondes, Jackie Robinson had to be on the lookout for rifle barrels. Threats assaulted his wife and son. Reporters assailed him with curveball questions. One that stung in particular was, "When do you think you're going to hit?"

Robinson, like many singular athletes, had a solitary temperament. But when he strode back from home plate after barely skimming the edge of his bat off a slider and the gush of insults dogged each step, Jackie Robinson looked singularly lonely, sitting off by himself three quarters of the way down the dugout bench.

Players in slumps often shrink from contact. They are in no mood to converse; their teammates don't want to catch whatever pox has made them malfunction (and rookies struggling to win jobs are quarantined). So Jackie Robinson sat apart from his teammates; it would be weeks before they would venture the few feet over to join him. Observing this distance—in the dugout, the locker room, and on the Dodger team bus—columnist Jimmy Cannon wrote, "He is the loneliest man I have ever seen in sports."

Yet other Dodgers were getting a small glimpse of his ordeals in their daily mail. Southerners on the team, especially Pee Wee Reese, received ugly scrawled notes from what seemed to be some of Robinson's most persistent correspondents, asking the Southerners, "How can you play with a nigger?"

Even as Robinson's hitting flagged, his baserunning

skills and daring drew attention in the stands. Attendance records, swelled by black families and church groups, followed the Dodgers as they moved west, through Pittsburgh, Cincinnati, Chicago, and St. Louis. Wendell Smith wrote:

> Jackie's nimble
> Jackie's quick
> Jackie's making the turnstiles click

Robinson's bunts, baserunning, and fielding kept him in the Brooklyn lineup until his bat could come around; by the first week of May, he had adjusted his eye and swing to connect against major league pitching. In the first ten games of May, he hit .395. Ben Chapman became so eager to pass himself off as a Robinson enthusiast that he made a point of telling reporters, "He's a major leaguer in every respect." But at that point, Chapman sounded only like the last to know. When the Dodgers came to Cincinnati in the middle of May, Jackie Robinson was welcomed as a guest with the rest of the team at the Netherlands Plaza Hotel. He could not eat in the dining room, but permitting blacks to stay behind closed doors was considered progress.

The Dodgers went on to Pittsburgh for a three-game series. Robinson stroked six hits in thirteen at bats. At one point he scratched a ground ball over to the left side of the infield and ran to beat the throw to first base.

Hank Greenberg, who had just been traded to the Pirates for his last year in the major leagues, stood staunchly on the bag. The most prominent Jew in major league baseball would not be pushed off; the first black player of the century in major league baseball would not be pushed away. The two men who knew most about the stain and sting of bigotry in baseball collided at first base on an afternoon in Forbes Field. The crunch rang out in both dugouts. An umpire called Robinson safe. Hank Greenberg rose slowly with the ball in his huge gloved hand. The two men smacked dust from their jerseys and resettled their caps on their heads. They each turned to watch the mound and began to crouch for the next pitch.

"Stick in there," Hank Greenberg called to Jackie Robinson behind him. "You're doing fine. Keep your chin up." After the game, Robinson told Wendell Smith, "Class sticks out all over Mr. Greenberg."

Pee Wee Reese was almost as fortunate in his own adversary. Branch Rickey had indulged Kirby Higbe's desire not to play on the same team as Jackie Robinson, and traded him to Pittsburgh. Higbe blamed Pee Wee Reese for first agreeing to be a part of the group that wanted to ban Jackie Robinson, then disowning the idea.

When Reese led off the Brooklyn batting order in the first inning, Kirby Higbe was on the mound against his old teammates. He cast the first stone at Pee Wee Reese's chin. Pee Wee flinched back, away from the pitch, and fell into the dirt. The umpire shook a warning finger at Higbe—only one beanball would be permitted. Higbe had to bring his next pitch over the plate, and Pee Wee, who was not a power hitter, swung from his heels and punched the ball into the right field bleachers. Branch Rickey's campaign of nonviolent resistance must have seemed awfully convincing as Reese made an uncommon home run trot around the bases.

The Dodgers went on to Chicago, where Cubs shortstop Len Merullo slipped back behind Robinson to take a pickoff throw. The two men went down in a mutual tumble. When Merullo pulled out his legs, he kicked Robinson on the outside of his right thigh. Robinson leapt up and drew back his right hand, then put it down at his side. The Dodgers wondered if Jackie had suddenly changed his mind, or just decided to change Merullo's.

New York's major newspapers were attentive to the importance of Jackie Robinson's arrival in the major leagues. But there was a conspicuous difference in awareness between the major dailies and the African-American press in covering the daily drip of racial taunts that dogged Robinson's every step. The *New York Times,* the *Herald-Tribune,* the *Daily News,* and *PM* covered the harassment when it became a police matter. But the day-to-day harrying, beanballs, and taunts usually passed without notice. The major dailies—even *PM*, Marshall Field's outspoken liberal daily, in which the utterances of Paul Robeson, Charlie Chaplin, and Henry Wallace resonated almost like scripture—rarely made race a major feature of the ongoing story of Jackie Robinson's entry into organized baseball.

Reading the daily newspapers now alongside histories and oral accounts can be frustrating. Reporting Robinson's season in hits, runs, and stolen bases seems to miss the real story by a wide mark. But it was only the residue of Branch Rickey's design. Rickey had sought to enlist reporters as partners in his social experiment. He felt that Robinson's best protection—and Brooklyn's—against getting scorched by some kind of dangerous racial melodrama was to write about Jackie Robinson as just another rookie Dodger.

Rickey's plan was audible night after night in the honeysuckle play-by-play of Red Barber from Ebbets Field. Two years before, Rickey had taken Barber to lunch and revealed his plan to integrate major league baseball with the Dodgers. Barber reacted as a white Mississippian of the times—he was aghast. But by the time Jackie Robinson actually donned a Brooklyn uniform, Barber had become comfortable in Flatbush, at Toots Shor's restaurant, and at being a personage around New York. He was willing to trade the attitudes of his

Mississippi youth for the prosperity and prominence he enjoyed in Brooklyn.

So when Jackie Robinson took the field, Red referred to him as "Robinson." Robinson, the rookie who had a sensational minor league season in Montreal. Robinson, *period*. It was never "Jackie Robinson, the first Negro in organized ball," "Robinson, the history-maker," or "Robinson, carrying the hopes and dreams of integration on his broad shoulders . . ." Just "Robinson." Robinson was a Bum, alongside Pee Wee, Dixie, and Furillo. It was, "Robinson looks at a fastball, low and outside, ball one . . ." until one day, casually, spontaneously, Barber called him "Robbie": "Robbie takes a lead off first . . . Robbie scrambles back . . ." "Robbie." A nickname from Red Barber was an honorific in Brooklyn.

Of course, race was the story in the black press. Jackie Robinson's arrival in major league baseball was not just the narrative of a brave man confronting racism. It was the shattering of a barrier that was, in its time, as forbidding as the Berlin Wall, and assumed to be just about as permanent. White newspapers probably grasped this. But that story would not sell—it did not hold the same urgent interest—among the majority of their readers.

. . .

June 1947 began with the front page of the *Daily News* declaring:

PREPARE FOR ATOM WAR, U.S. WARNED

But that could have been a headline of almost any day. Pete Reiser crashed into Ebbets Field's center field wall catching a ball and cracked his shoulder. He held onto the ball; the Dodgers held on to win, 9–4. But Branch Rickey was criticized for being too cheap to install rubber padding along the outfield walls. On June 5, Reiser followed the game from his hospital room while Brooklyn beat the Pirates 3–0 and Jackie Robinson stole his eighth base of the season.

The umpires association in Washington, D.C., refused to provide umpires for a game between a local naval air station and a naval reserve team because the air station had a black pitcher. Washington was an American League city (an incongruous name, under the circumstances), so Brooklyn did not have to worry about playing in the nation's capital (which also seemed an incongruous title). That weekend, the largest crowd of the season filled Ebbets, and saw Jackie Robinson steal two more bases against the St. Louis Cardinals and score two runs.

Robinson told Sam Lacy in an interview, "I often prefer to be alone. That's true. They often invite me into card games when we're traveling and there's always a word of encouragement when I fail to deliver in the pinch. When I make a particularly good play, they slap me on the back or grab my hand. I couldn't ask for any more."

Lacey ended his column saying, "Frankly, I think the time for concern about Jackie is over."

But being included in team camaraderie had other hazards. Robinson was invited to join the long card games that filled the Dodgers' train trips west. One of the mainstays of such games was Hugh Casey, the relief pitcher from Georgia. Casey had been one of the first Dodgers to offer a hand to Jackie Robinson. He batted balls to him during practice to help Jackie learn the terrain around first base. He ran a restaurant in Brooklyn, and proudly displayed a signed photo of Robinson behind the bar. But Hugh Casey was a jolly man who would have a lick too much of liquor and then something ugly and silly would drop out of his mouth. He would drink while he played cards, and played cards to drink. Once, after folding a hand, he reached across the cards and rubbed Robinson's head. "I got to change my luck, Jackie," he said. "In Georgia, when my poker luck got bad. I'd just go out and rub me the teat of the biggest, blackest nigger woman I could find."

Robinson's speechlessness summoned the most restraint he had to muster all year.*

---

* Hugh Casey would shoot himself three years later, at the age of thirty-eight.

• • •

On June 14, Robinson began a batting streak that would run for twenty-one straight games. He had raised his average to .315, and was leading the league in stolen bases. Newspapers began to acclaim the sense of drama he could lend a game simply by drawing a walk and dancing off first base to a pitcher's distraction. "The Black Meteor" became one nickname. "The Bojangles of the Basepaths" caught on less.

At the same time, as one unnamed opposing player told Dick Young of the *Daily News,* "Jackie Robinson can usually count on the first pitch being right under his nostrils." By midseason, he had been hit seven times, more than any other player had been hit during the entire 1946 season. And that figure did not reflect the number of beanings Robinson averted by being able to bail out of the batter's box so quickly. To reporters, he professed that he was almost grateful to have a bead drawn on his chin. He said during his batting slump, "Since I can't buy a hit, they're doing me a favor."

The brushback pitches began to decline once pitchers and managers realized that hitting Jackie Robinson only gave the most dazzling base runner in baseball a staging area on first base. Whatever satisfaction a pitcher might get from plunking Jackie Robinson in the ribs would be quickly diminished once Robinson stole second base behind his back.

• • •

The next day the Dodgers were on their way to Chicago for a three-game series and stopped in Danville, Illinois, to play an exhibition against one of their farm clubs. The morning of the game, Pee Wee Reese, Harold Parrott, pitcher Rex Barney, and Roscoe McGowan of the *New York Times* formed a golf foursome. Before teeing off on an early hole, Pee Wee saw Robinson and Wendell Smith on the green just behind them. Reese held up his group and called out to Robinson and Smith to join them.

Wendell noticed that the three players joshed and gossiped with one another about baseball, and the reporters and the Dodger executive griped among themselves about the foibles of small-town hotels. The black and white differences seemed less significant than the distinction between players and onlookers.

The friendship with Pee Wee Reese so enshrined today mostly developed after that first season, when Robinson was moved to second base and the two became an accomplished double play tandem. When the Dodger infield posed for pictures on the dugout steps, the taller Robinson usually rested his right elbow casually on Pee Wee's left shoulder. Reese would often slide his left arm behind Robinson's back.

Bogie and Bacall, gin and vermouth, Hope and Crosby—Reese and Robinson.

In fact, the two men had different recollections of the first moment they remembered Pee Wee coming across the infield to extend an encouraging arm around his friend's shoulder. Pee Wee thought it came early in the season in Cincinnati, when scores of assorted Reese relatives drove across the Ohio River from Kentucky to hear jerks in the stands jeer Robinson for being a black man insolent enough to play with whites, and hiss at Reese for playing alongside him. Robinson remembered the moment as occurring in Boston, where the crowds could be particularly vicious, and close enough so that Robinson could hear whole sentences of slurs, not just blunt single-word epithets. Years later, Robinson wrote, "Pee Wee didn't answer them. Without a glance in their direction, he left his position and walked over to me. His words weren't important. I don't even remember what he said. It was the gesture of comradeship and support that counted."

Whenever the moment happened—and more likely, the gesture became so familiar and accepted that each man became aware of it at the time it meant the most to him—it signaled that the two Dodgers had acquired a stake in one another.

• • •

The Dodgers got to Chicago and defeated the Cubs at Wrigley, 5–3. Robinson singled in the seventh inning, got moved along to second by Gene Hermanski's sacrifice bunt, then kept churning when he noticed that Stan Hack had left third to cover the bunt. Robinson reached third before the throw whistled past the abandoned base, and then just kept on going. He scored a run from first on a sacrifice bunt.

The next day, Robinson hit half a home run. That is, in the sixth inning he drew a walk, danced off first, and annoyed pitcher Johnny Schmitz so meticulously that he threw over to first nine times, trying to keep Robinson close. Schmitz finally threw a pitch to Pee Wee Reese, but half his mind and most of his arm strength had already been spent on Robinson. Pee Wee hit his fat, flat pitch into Wrigley's right center field, scoring two runs to cinch Brooklyn's victory.

On June 20, Bugsy Siegel was shot through the living room window of his home in Hollywood. The *Daily News* strongly suggested that he was a workmanlike New York thug who had been tempted and corrupted by show business. They headlined:

A GOOD HOOD GONE HOLLYWOOD

• • •

On June 24, Jackie Robinson stole home.

It was the first time Robinson would make the play for which he became most famous. Every detail in the design of baseball tilts against a player stealing home. After all, home is where the pitcher throws the ball. A runner who dares to try to steal home gambles that he can run down the third base line quicker than a pitcher can speed the ball to exactly the same spot. The move astonishes because it seems to make as much sense as jumping off the Golden Gate Bridge—if you're safe, it's an accident. Such is the play that became the signature of Jackie Robinson's career.

It was the fifth inning of a game against the Pirates; Pittsburgh was ahead 2–1. Robinson drew a walk from Fritz Ostermueller. There were two outs. A walk that put even Jackie Robinson three bases away from scoring seemed more like a nuisance than a threat. But Carl Furillo looped a single into short left field, and when Ralph Kiner had to run in to pluck up the ball, Robinson kept steaming. He legged his way into third.

Dixie Walker came up next for the Dodgers. Ostermueller was a left-handed pitcher. To keep Furillo close at first, Ostermueller had to pitch from the stretch, which turned his back toward Robinson on third. Jack danced a few inches off the base, but the risk he posed from there seemed small. When Ostermueller wound into his third pitch, Robinson broke for home. But within a few feet, he put on a heel-screeching stop. The

Pittsburgh catcher, Dixie Howell (baseball is the only sport in which half the principals in a play are likely to be named Dixie), held onto the ball and stared Robinson back to third. It appeared as if the Black Meteor had almost flamed out.

But Robinson's sprint of inches had not been a blunder. His supposed missteps had enabled Carl Furillo to run to second. And it meant that Ostermueller would revert to his usual full, looping windup because there were two outs and no base left open to steal. Or so it seemed.

Without so much as a glance toward Jackie Robinson, Fritz Ostermueller reared back to fire his next pitch past Dixie Walker. And Jackie Robinson broke for home.

The crowd clacked like a chorus of geese. Ostermueller caught the sound, but could not stop his windup without committing a balk—which would bring Robinson home. He teetered for just a moment on his right toe, then hurled the ball low, to the right side of the plate. The pitch beat Robinson home, of course, but it drew Dixie Howell off to the far side of the plate. Robinson hit full speed as quickly as a cheetah. He sawed off half a dozen quick sprinter's strides, then used the last to propel himself into a slide, curling his right leg into a hook that snagged the prow of home plate before Dixie Howell could get his heavy glove over to Robinson's foot. The umpire barked "Safe!" Brooklyn went ahead.

The Dodgers won, 4–2, bringing them into first place, where they were to stay for the rest of the season.*

On July 4, Bill Veeck signed Larry Doby of the Newark Eagles to a contract with the Cleveland Indians, making Doby the second black major league player of the twentieth century. He was to get much of the same grief, but not half the eventual acclaim.

Five bull terriers bit an eleven-year-old boy to death in the Bronx. A U.S. Air Force commander said that for reasons of national security, he could not allow photographers to snap pictures of the remnants of wreckage in Roswell, New Mexico, but it looked to him like the bits and pieces of a silvery weather balloon. In Dayton, Ohio, Orville of the Wright brothers said, "UFOs are propaganda dished up by the government to support the current State Department campaign to get us into another war."

_____

* Although the play became Robinson's signature of daring, he stole home only nine times in his career. Ty Cobb, by comparison, stole home fifty-four times. Pete Reiser, Robinson's teammate, stole home seven times in 1946 alone. But the play has been fading from modern baseball. The Cardinals' great Lou Brock stole 938 bases in his career, but home just twice. Power hitters have been distributed up and down most batting orders. Why should anyone on the modern New York Yankees dare to try to steal home when Bernie Williams, Derek Jeter, and Jason Giambi are coming up?

• • •

Jackie Robinson's face began to appear in several national magazine ads. He urged readers to buy Bond Bread and Old Gold Cigarettes although, he confirmed for reporters, he did not smoke. His standard rookie salary, supplemented by a signing bonus from Mr. Rickey and the new advertising income, made Robinson the third-highest-paid player in baseball in 1947.

In mid-July, the Kiwanis Club of Ahoskie, North Carolina, held a lottery for a Cadillac, and a U.S. Navy veteran named Harvey Jones drew the winning ticket. Mr. Jones was black. The Kiwanians said they could not award him the car; they offered to give back the dollar he had paid for the raffle ticket. Carmen Cavallaro, the local orchestra leader who had drawn the ticket, refused to draw another, as did the band's vocalist, Leslie Long, who added, "Race and color don't mean a thing, especially in music." The Ahoskie club reversed itself and said Mr. Jones would get the car he had won. But then dealer Charles Jenkins said he couldn't find the car he had promised to give away.

That same day, the American League's St. Louis Browns signed Henry Thompson and Willard Brown of the Kansas City Monarchs.

• • •

New York was not North Carolina. Of course not. But on July 29, the Supreme Court of New York said that the Stuyvesant Town apartment complex being built by Metropolitan Life between First Avenue and Avenue C in lower Manhattan could exclude black families. Private developers, said the court, can "restrict such accommodations on grounds of race, color, creed, or religion."

In August, fighting intensified between Arabs and Jews in Palestine. On August 18, the Dodgers opened a series with the St. Louis Cardinals, and Joe Medwick spiked Jackie Robinson high on his shin on a play at first base. Robinson's shin was several inches from the bag; what business Joe Medwick's shoe had in the vicinity was not apparent.

Two days later, Enos Slaughter of the Cardinals stabbed a similar wound eight inches above Robinson's ankle. The Dodgers bounded out of the dugout as a team—Hugh Casey was in the lead—to shout for the umpires to throw Slaughter out of the game. Slaughter said, with palpable and practiced sincerity, that he never spiked anyone. Some of his teammates offered a more plausible argument: that if Enos Slaughter had meant to slash Jackie Robinson, Robinson would have left the game on a stretcher.

The Dodgers split the two-game series, and pulled four games ahead of the Cardinals. Looking for late-season relief pitching, Branch Rickey signed Dan Bankhead from the Negro League Memphis Stars. But Wendell Smith remained Jackie Robinson's roommate.

The Dodgers and Cardinals played another critical series that began on September 12. Joe Garagiola, the St. Louis catcher, hit a double-play ball to Pee Wee Reese and tried to beat the throw at first base. His spikes came down on Jackie Robinson's heel. When Robinson came to bat in the third inning, he said something to Garagiola, who, gregarious even then, returned Robinson's commentary with some force. Umpire Beans Reardon stepped between the two men barking at each other, one white, one black, and commanded them to play ball. Then an astonishing thing happened: nothing more.

The next day, the *Sporting News* named Jackie Robinson the 1947 Rookie of the Year. A newswire photo showed Jackie playing cards on a bed in a St. Louis hotel room with Pee Wee, Ralph Branca, and Eddie Stanky. But the photograph was clearly staged: no money was visible.

On September 19, the Memphis Censorship Board banned the children's movie *Curley* because it showed black and white children playing together. Lloyd Binford, chairman of the Memphis Board of Censors wrote to the film's producer, "I am sorry to have to inform you that we are unable to approve your *Curley* picture with the little Negroes, as the South does not permit Negroes in white schools nor recognize social equality between the races, even in children."

Producer Hal Roach wrote back, "Will you ban newspapers that show photographs of the Brooklyn Dodgers?"

In the morning newspapers of September 20, New Yorkers learned that Rita Hayworth had sued Orson Welles for divorce and that the American Association of Scientific Workers said bacterial warfare could be a bigger threat to the world than the atom bomb. President Truman asked Americans not to eat meat on Tuesdays, or eggs and poultry on Thursdays.

In the middle of the morning, the city learned that former Mayor Fiorello La Guardia had died of cancer in the Bronx.

The city put on mourning stripes for the man who had seemed to embody so much of the city's pluck, grit, wit, diversity, and audacity. Flags were lowered. Crêpe was draped over the windows at City Hall, and unfurled over the entrances of every public school, fire house, police station, and Catholic church.

The Dodgers had won the pennant and their train was returning from the wilds of St. Louis. Dodger officials had heard the news of La Guardia's death, and assumed that it would discourage a crowd from gathering to greet them at Penn Station. Even Branch Rickey—particularly Branch Rickey—would be in mourning for the former mayor.

The Dodgers' train pulled into Pennsylvania Station shortly before six at night. Thousands of fans had crammed into the station. Thousands of people had seemed to decide that the 1947 Dodgers had, in a way, won a battle for the city that Fiorello La Guardia had opened with his intrepid calls for justice and equity, tolerance and gallantry. The Jackie Robinson Dodgers, with their assortment of Southerners, Sicilians, and blacks, had become a kind of Fusion ticket. Fans lined the platforms alongside the tracks. They mobbed the waiting rooms and snaked up the stairs into the grand marble terminal. Pee Wee Reese's feet did not so much as scuff those floors. Fans lifted him from the train's steps onto their shoulders, and carried the Dodgers shortstop out to Seventh Avenue.

Dodgers officials had worried about what threats crowds, even happy ones, could conceal that might endanger Jackie Robinson. So they brought him down from a rear car of the train, and thought to bring him out from behind, after most of the throngs had filed out. But Jackie stopped to make a phone call. He phoned Rachel to say, "Hi, honey, I'm back, we won the pennant, be home soon." As he stood in the phone booth, Jackie Robinson was recognized.

A swarm of Dodgers fans, most of them white, surrounded the phone booth. They cheered for Jackie, and when he shouted back his thanks and politely asked for a moment of quiet so he could speak to his wife, they cheered Rachel Robinson, too. Laughing, he tried to come out, but the folding door was shut by a crush of adulation. Police moved in. Several patrolmen parted a path for the best base runner in baseball.

"Where are you going, Jackie?" they asked. He and Wendell Smith wanted to find a cab. The crush around them tightened.

"No," the officers said, "where are you going?" They made room in the front seat of a police car. A motorcade of Dodgers, blue uniforms, and a few fans threaded their way down Seventh Avenue toward the Brooklyn Bridge. They clipped past blinking signs shouting blunt neon slogans—"COFFEE" "PIZZA" "BAGELS" "BIALYS" "BEAUTIFUL GIRLS" "BAR & GRILL"—past stone honeycombs of office lights, and headed into the starry boulevards winking on and off in Brooklyn Heights, Williamsburg, Cobble Hill, and Red Hook, and a sliver of Queens beyond.

9

Epilogue

There is no need for a new chronicle about Jackie Robinson's arrival in major league baseball. But it has been my privilege to try to tell one. The Robinson story has become a kind of American parable. It shares shelf space in our minds along with Mr. Lincoln, the Railsplitter, coming out of the prairies to fell slavery; the Lone Eagle, Lindbergh, vaulting across the Atlantic to announce the arrival of America; and Franklin D. Roosevelt rising from the despair of polio to put steel in the spine of a nation. It is the story of a solitary American man of conviction who stands a head taller and strides out boldly alone, to smite hate, ignorance, or fear.

The World Series of 1947 was thrilling. Bill Bevens of the Yankees was one out from pitching the first no-hitter in series history in the fourth game when Cookie Lavagetto of the Dodgers hit a double to score two runs and win the round for Brooklyn.

But the Yankees won the series, 4 games to 3. Jackie Robinson was the Most Valuable Player in the National League in 1949, but the Dodgers lost the World Series to the Yankees again. Brooklyn avoided that annual ignominy in 1951 by losing the famous one-game playoff to the New York Giants. Jackie Robinson trailed Bobby Thompson around the bases on his home run trot, like some kind of hawk, while his teammates filed slowly off the field in shock at their last-second defeat; Jackie was still in the game, ready to cry out if Thompson had missed a base. The Dodgers came back to the World Series again in 1952, and lost to the Yankees; and did so again in 1953. In 1955, Brooklyn finally won its first—and what would prove to be the borough's only—World Series. The players were lauded with a parade, watches, silver sets, and pledges of undying love and gratitude. Three years later, the team lit out for Los Angeles.

Branch Rickey lost a struggle with Brooklyn Trust executives over the Dodgers, and packed off for Pittsburgh. Walter O' Malley—a name you don't say aloud in parts of Brooklyn even today—traded Jackie Robinson to the Giants, but Robinson chose to retire. He found that he couldn't lift a bat against Brooklyn, and his circulation, aggravated by stress and the early stages of diabetes, was worse than perhaps he even knew. New York Giants president Horace Stoneham wrote Jackie a wistful, charming note in his own hand: "All of us wish you success and happiness in your new career but I can't help thinking it would have been fun to have you on our side for a year or two."

The story of the wound left open in Brooklyn by the flight of the Dodgers has become a sad ballad, usually sung to make an unexceptional point: big-time sports is ultimately an unsentimental, bottom-line business like making shoes, steel, or men's suits. Those industries also left Brooklyn.

Today, at least baseball is back. The minor league Brooklyn Cyclones play in a button-cute stadium in Coney Island. The swell of development in Brooklyn over the past decade may now give the borough an economic base and fan profile that would make it a better bet for success than most of the smaller places proposed for major league expansion. But for the moment, baseball in Brooklyn is a boutique item.

It would be heartening to report that Jackie Robinson saw the brunt of American bigotry in 1947 and never again was taunted, spiked, or threatened. But while the ferocity and frequency of such attacks fluctuated, they never quite halted. Manager Burt Shotten showed an ugly scrawled scrap of a note to his players in the locker room before a game against the St. Louis Cardinals in 1953: "Robinson, you die, no use crying for the cops. You will be executed gangland-style in Busch Stadium." When the team walked out, distracted, to take their warmup drill, Robinson took up his accustomed position next to Reese. "Not so close, Jack, please," said Pee Wee.

Scores of black players came into organized baseball after Jackie Robinson broke that trail in 1947. Many of them (in minor league Southern towns especially) faced the same daily assault of taunts and beanballs. Many, including Larry Doby, Monte Irvin, Willie Mays, and Roy Campanella, were capable of the same unflinching valor as Robinson if they had been called to the challenge. But because Jackie Robinson fought the first battle, they had his example before them.

Robinson was shrewd enough about himself to know that the combativeness that would later mark his relationship with many reporters (even Wendell Smith would come to write about his "prickliness," a lightly disguised code word) would work against his early election to the Hall of Fame. But it didn't. He was elected, virtually unanimously, in 1962, and presented by Branch Rickey.

Over the years, some revisionist sports historians and columnists have argued that Branch Rickey's motive for undertaking his "experiment" was strictly self-serving. It is unnecessary to dispute the charge. It is only curious as to why it is presented as some kind of revelation. Rickey's own words were consistently blunt and unapologetic. "I want to win the pennant, Jackie," he told him on their first meeting in August 1945, "and we need ballplayers to do it. Do you think you can do it?" Any purpose that claimed to be more praiseworthy, patriotic, or socially progressive would have been distrusted.

There is no longer any serious lobby in the United States for segregation in sports. But a criticism from a new perspective has been offered over the past generation by some thinkers and activists (Amiri Baraka may be the most prominent) who believe that the integration of baseball, of which Jackie Robinson was the forerunner, typified what they see as the folly of integration. They point out that before Jackie Robinson, hundreds of black players, coaches, and owners earned a living in baseball, principally in the Negro Leagues. After integration, it was only dozens—the Negro Leagues died.*

The integration of baseball that is visible on the field of

---

* There was a similar, though not total, deterioration of various Latin American leagues, in which blacks and Latinos had played for meager wages, but free from any apprehension that they would be signed by a rich American major league team.

155

almost any game in the United States is still not reflected in the ranks of managers and coaches, much less in the skybox suites of owners.

The push for integration that became U.S. national policy in the 1960s and 1970s seems to show mixed results. So many public schools in major league cities that were desegregated by demonstrations and court decisions have become essentially resegregated, and the quality of public education in America's inner cities has not been notably improved.

But the past generation has rearranged America's racial landscape. Integration is no longer a goal, it is a fact that has penetrated into the daily lives of millions. Not only Americans who live and work in mixed-ethnic settings, but citizens with mixed families that cannot be neatly defined by the categories on a census form.

Even if you accept the doubtful proposition of some revisionist activists that the Negro Leagues could have been sustained past 1960, what fields would be open—or closed—to a star like Derek Jeter, from a mixed ethnic family? Would there have to be a separate league for the Hispanic stars who have, from Pedro Martinez to Sammy Sosa to Luis Gonzales, almost dominated organized baseball in some seasons? And then another for emerging Asian stars?

The success of integration has been imperfect. But it no longer reflects idealism. It reveals what has become the gorgeously varied complexion of America.

• • •

When the U.S. military was integrated in 1948, those who argued that mixing blacks, whites, and Hispanics in the barracks would sow discord in the ranks had to answer the argument, "What about Jackie Robinson and the Brooklyn Dodgers?"

Rosa Parks refusing to surrender her seat on a Montgomery bus; children in Birmingham daring the dank jails so they could grow up to go to good schools and drink out of public water fountains; civil rights pioneers marching uprightly into torrential water cannon and snarling dogs; Colin Powell becoming the most admired American—none of that can be traced directly to Jackie Robinson trudging out, alone and assailed, under a hail of taunts. But because he made that walk, millions of Americans could bear the memory of his heroism in their minds as they searched for the courage to keep striving.

The day-to-day story of Jackie Robinson's entry into baseball brought Americans face to face with the question of race at the breakfast table. It was resourcefully disguised as a discussion about balls, strikes, and stolen bases, whites, blacks, and Dodger blue.

One way to observe the impact his story had on America is to see the way in which Jackie Robinson sharpened his own life.

The man who had once appraised his being by runs, hits, and errors became an activist, a columnist, a businessman, an agitator, and a community conscience. By the time he was elected to the Hall of Fame, reporters were more likely to ask him about the Voting Rights Act than how to hit right-handed pitching. Jackie Robinson agitated for overturning segregation, stimulating black investment, hiring black managers, and giving youngsters greater opportunity. He ferociously opposed racial separation, anti-Semitism, and being told to go slow in the march for justice.

He admired Martin Luther King, Pee Wee Reese, Ralph Bunche, Branch Rickey, and Nelson Rockefeller. He marched with King in Birmingham and Washington, played golf with Pee Wee, worked for Rockefeller, and revered Ralph Bunche and Branch Rickey.

Not all of the adversaries Jackie Robinson acquired were as small-minded as Ben Chapman. Robinson admired Paul Robeson (actor, athlete, attorney, activist, singer, scholar—one of the few men who did more things well than Jackie Robinson) for risking his career and comfort to advance the socialist principles he believed would benefit black Americans. But he reproached Robeson for being naïve about the Stalinist crimes of the Soviet Union. He admired Malcolm X in his calls for black pride and self-reliance. But he upbraided Malcolm and the Black Muslims for being absent from the battlegrounds in Alabama and Mississippi where blacks—and whites—were risking their lives to win social justice.

"You mouth a big and bitter battle, Malcolm," Robinson wrote in his column in the *Amsterdam News*, "but it is noticeable that your militancy is mainly expressed in Harlem where it is safe."

Robinson thought that Adam Clayton Powell Jr. was a rogue and a crook. Powell's supporters did not disagree, and cared even less. But Jackie defended the Harlem politician when Congress unseated him. Perhaps playing with the likes of Hugh Casey and Leo Durocher had convinced Robinson that rascals could be put to good purposes.

Jackie Robinson became an active Republican. He believed that free enterprise was a feature of freedom. Being a New York Republican meant supporting Nelson Rockefeller and Jacob Javitz, who supported the civil rights movement, while Confederate Democrats like Richard Russell and Strom Thurmond filibustered against it.

Robinson endorsed Richard Nixon for president in 1960 after he met with Jack Kennedy and found his commitment to civil rights listless. That analysis still seems sound. But Robinson cooled on Nixon when the vice president refused to call for Martin Luther King's release from the Birmingham jail. And he became icy when the party nominated Barry Goldwater in 1964, who had voted against civil rights bills. Robinson refused to endorse Goldwater, saying the party had abandoned blacks.

Would American politics have been different over the past thirty years if Jackie Robinson had been around to remind Republicans of their first stirrings as the party of civil rights? And to admonish Democrats not to take the votes of blacks for granted?

Still, Jackie Robinson was an athlete.

Among the millennial polls that appeared in 1999 were ones for Athlete of the 20th Century. Muhammad Ali, Michael Jordan, and Babe Ruth were usually at the top. All three were completely accomplished in their realms.

Ali could not only float like a butterfly and sting like a bee, he could take a punch like a brick. Michael Jordan blocked shots as well as he scored points. Babe Ruth, it is sometimes forgotten, was a record-setting pitcher before he ever hit home runs, and even a nimble base runner until his body got bloated by sauerbraten and beer. All three were superb practicing psychologists who unnerved their opponents with rope-a-dope, trash talking, and calling home run shots.

Ali never applied himself to a sport other than boxing. Hats or helmets would have concealed his pretty face. Michael Jordan's effort to become a major league ballplayer was serious and preposterous. Babe Ruth played golf to drink martinis.

But baseball, the game he so distinguished, was not even Jackie Robinson's best sport. He was the finest college basketball forward on the West Coast. He would have been favored to win the 1940 Olympic decathlon if the games had not been cancelled by war. He was one of the supreme college running backs of all time (no other man is in both the Baseball and College Football Halls of Fame).

Jackie Robinson even won a Ping-Pong championship.

Many athletes find that the critical difference between performers of equal ability is the skill to succeed under stress. Ali, Jordan, and Ruth all had to surpass the unreasonable expectation to be not only good, but magical. Ali had the added load of fighting a court case that could break him while it made him the object of incomparable veneration.

But none of that compares to the weight Jackie Robinson carried onto the field: the threat of his own death; the fear for his family; the taunts, catcalls, beanballs, brushback pitches, high spikes, and low blows; and finally, trying to play ball while worrying that history could turn—or be turned back—by whether he could hit a curve, and not hit back at his tormentors.

• • •

Robinson's last years were afflicted with trials. The walk of a man who once was fast enough to beat a pitch to home plate became hobbled and halting as his circulation clogged. His sharp eyes became so strained that he often turned off the lights, drew the blinds, and sat in gloom.

His oldest son, Jack Jr., became a soldier, went to Vietnam, and brought home a drug habit. When his son was arrested in a drug den with several pounds of heroin and a gun, Jackie Robinson suffered a wound no slur or spike had ever opened. But he didn't back away from reporters on the courthouse steps, telling them, "I haven't had much effect on anyone's child if I didn't have much on my own."

Jack Robinson Jr. bravely battled back from drugs. He was helping to run the recovery center that had helped restore his life when he fell asleep at the wheel of a car after working through the night and smashed into a guardrail. People who say that Jackie Robinson died a year later at the age of fifty-three because he was finally broken by the cruel, dumb weight of a thousand insults, beanballs, and thorns may forget that no grief cuts deeper than that of a parent who must hold a dead child. Jackie Robinson gave his life for something great, and then moved on.

Acknowledgments, Notes, and Thanks

A daughter of Brooklyn, Kee Malesky, has researched, proofread, and improved virtually everything I have written for publication, and much of what I have broadcast for a number of years I would trust only her to confirm. Kee brought particular dedication to this story of a moment that ennobled Brooklyn and improved the entire country. What cannot be improved upon is the debt of gratitude I owe Kee each week.

This book was completed with no approval or cooperation from Jackie Robinson's family. Rachel Robinson sent back word through the estimable Jackie Robinson Foundation that she did not choose to speak with me. She is involved in many worthy projects, and we are fortunate that she has been able to share her own extraordinary story in her own books and commemorations. Their children, Sharon Robinson in New York and David

Robinson, now living in Tanzania, also chose not to participate.

The story of Jackie Robinson's arrival is compelling material for an author, and I am indebted to many who have preceded me with much more complete volumes. Arnold Rampersad's *Jackie Robinson: A Biography* (Ballantine Books, 1997) and Jules Tygiel's *Baseball's Great Experiment: Jackie Robinson and his Legacy* (Oxford University Press, 1983) are the classic and indispensable works. They trace the story from Jackie Robinson's early life through his collegiate and army career, his baseball life, and his final incarnation as a community and civil rights personage and American hero. They both draw on incomparable interviews and access to Jackie Robinson's papers. Maury Allen's *Jackie Robinson: A Life Remembered* (Franklin Watts, 1987), offers engaging and good recollections from people who played alongside and against him. David Falkner's *Great Time Coming: The Life of Jackie Robinson from Baseball to Birmingham* (Simon & Schuster, 1995) is a solid and informative retelling of the story.

Jackie Robinson himself was the co-author of two autobiographies. The first, *My Own Story,* as told to Wendell Smith (Greenberg, 1948) rather clearly reflects Robinson's enthusiasm about succeeding in major league baseball. In recalling some of his trials, Robinson is more of a diplomat than a diarist—a wise and honorable perspective from someone who was still an active player.

The book co-authored with Al Duckett, *I Never Had It Made* (Putnam, 1972) is more vivid on this and other scores, and reflects Robinson's growing annoyance with major league baseball's slogging pace of integration, especially of the ranks of coaches and managers. The first volume has the flavor of a banquet speech. The second is a more reflective work that conveys Robinson's various frustrations in baseball, business, and politics, as well as his maturation as a public figure.

I also found the 1950 motion picture *The Jackie Robinson Story* interesting for the poise Robinson brings to his own portrayal of himself. I have chosen to rely on Robinson's own interpretation of his meeting with Branch Rickey. I cannot imagine a Hollywood screenwriter or director persuading him to strike any false poses in depicting that critical occasion.

The Jackie Robinson Reader: Perspectives on an American Hero, edited by Jules Tygiel (Dutton, 1997), offers valuable reflections on Robinson's impact and larger import. *It Happened in Brooklyn: An Oral History of Growing Up in the Borough in the 1940s, 1950s, and 1960s,* by Myrna Katz Frommer and Harvey Frommer (Harcourt Brace & Company, 1993), provided an abundance of particular physical details from the lives of Brooklynites and Dodger fans of the 1940s.

My wife, Caroline Richard, and I tried to follow the 1947 baseball season, from spring training to the World Series, day by day in the microfilmed pages of the *New*

York Times, New York Daily News, New York Post, PM,
and the *New York Herald-Tribune.* The experience
confirmed for us that the *Herald-Tribune* was the most
distinguished newspaper in the city at that time—and that
the reporting of the big-city dailies differed critically from
the reporting and columns of Wendell Smith and Sam
Lacey in the black press of the time, principally the *Pittsburgh Courier,* the *Chicago Daily Defender,* and the
Baltimore Afro-American.

I am particularly grateful for the work of Wendell
Smith. I was fortunate to meet Wendell Smith several
times when I was a youngster. He was the first sports-
writer from the black press to be hired by a major city
daily, the *Chicago American,* and hosted a late-night
sportscast on WGN in Chicago. I would see him when
my father, Ernie Simon, came to those same studios to do
late-night car commercials.

Wendell and my father bore a notable resemblance to
each other. They were both expansive men with similarly
neat black moustaches, who dressed with similar flourish—except that my father, the Jew, might have been a
shade darker than Wendell, the black man. Whenever my
father had me in tow, jokes about my possible parentage
were irresistible. "Hiya doin', son of mine?" Wendell
would lean down and say. "Tell your mom my check is
on the way." He was a warm-spirited man who did not
have to be coaxed to talk about his old roommate,
Jackie Robinson. I only wish I had been older, and better

able to appreciate his wealth of recollection. As it is, Wendell's papers, which are now part of the Jackie Robinson collection at the Library of Congress, and his accumulated dispatches, articles, and columns, are precious and perceptive accounts of a historical passage.

Mark Reese was gracious and forthcoming with memories of his father, Pee Wee, and the times addressed in this volume. And my treasured colleague, Bob Edwards, kindly shared his matchless knowledge about Red Barber and his role in these events.

I am grateful to the staff of the incomparable Rose Room of New York's Public Library for giving me free run of their collection—a courtesy that is extended only to each person who enters that irreplaceable institution.

Another daughter of Brooklyn—by way of Normandy, Sonoma, and Manhattan—found herself caught up in this account of a departed baseball team's most affecting star. Brooklyn is where I first fell in love with Caroline Richard, at a party on Vanderbilt Avenue, and then as we ranged around Coney Island. We had our first date in the first days of the 2000 baseball season. We were married a month before the World Series. Now *that's* a great season.

When the events of September 11, 2001, struck, Caroline undertook research trips that the news kept me from making. She carried out these explorations with astuteness and growing fascination. This book had to be completed during a time in which Jackie Robinson's archives had been transmitted to the Library of Congress and were closed to the public while being prepared for display. But Caroline's earnestness and charm convinced Adrienne Cannon, Afro-American History Specialist at the Library of Congress, to open the collection for her perusal. I am grateful to Ms. Cannon. I thank Caroline for giving me a new life.

I write this while on assignment in Afghanistan with my longtime collaborator and friend, Peter Breslow, who has surely earned time off for good behavior. But I cherish his companionship and partnership.

I want to offer a last thanks to our collaborators on the ground here in Kabul, M. Shafi Moorzi and Zalmi Yawar. They are far more knowledgeable about America than I am about their country, in which we have been received with friendship. Shafi and Zalmi are a little blurry about the rules of baseball—an intelligent reaction. However, they can recognize courage, and they admire America. I close with a hope that the tragedy that fractured so many lives on September 11, 2001, all the same opened a door in history that will give Shafi, Zalmi, and their friends and families a chance to create the kind of society that deserves their goodness and bravery.

SSS
February 2002
Kabul, Afghanistan